Finding Acceptable Balance

To change the scale you must first change your mind.

By *Clarissa Young*

Paperback ISBN
9781687568762

Table of Content

Dedication

To my 1st True Love, my oldest son Tyler:

Being your mom has been one of the greatest gifts to me. Thanks for being my initial motivation to live life. As a result of me living for you, I now also have an awesome husband and 3 other beautiful children that I must live for. To my husband, I love you dearly and I thank you for all of the love and support that you provide to me and our children.

To you 4 and myself, I promise to continue to thrive to be in the best of health!

Loving you all dearly!

-Mommy/Wifey

Acknowledgments

To my pastor, Prophet Verna Du Pont I want to thank you for all the spiritual guidance that you provide to me. You have truly helped me to trust in God with every aspect of my life, including my health! Without my faith I know, I would not have made it this far on my fitness journey.

To my book mentor, Coach Chanell Fair I want to say thank you for helping me to make my dream of being a published author a reality.

To my launch team Alexis Evans, Lisa Jones, Dianna Jones, Diana Wilson, Melody Maxwell, Natalie Cunningham, Naomi Gomez, Karla Boggs, and Ramona Jemison for being the first to read my book and provide me with your honest feedback!

To my friends and family near and far I thank you and I love you for all of your support!

Last but certainly not least I want to say Thank You and I love all of my FABS for your continuous support, encouragement, and love. This is truly a complete circle of support; you motivate me, and I motivate you!

Love,

Rissa -Your Published Author Whoop Whoop!!!

To my readers,

Welcome to the family. You are officially a FABS (Finding Acceptable Balance Sister/Supporter). FABS are people that believe in me enough to join me on my journey. This makes a complete circle of support. I provide motivation, knowledge, and support to you. In return, your presence is what helps fuel my fight to be a better me. In life, we will face many obstacles. Those obstacles sometimes become more manageable when we have support. So, whether you're a FAB for purchasing this book, joining me on my journey, or following me on social media, I love you. You are appreciated!

I hope with this book you are able to read it, enjoy it, get to know me more, and find your F.A.B. If you let it, society will put you in many boxes. However, it's up to you to find what works for you. You are not to compare or try to mimic your life with anyone else. What works for your friend or family member may not work for you. You are special! You are unique! You are called by God and you were not meant to be put in a box of normalities. So as you read my book be brave, be bold, and most importantly be you. In doing so, I know you will learn some great tips to help you love "YOU" as you pursue your journey to having better health. Remember, It's not about the numbers on the scale. It is about having joy and living a healthy happy life, for as long as you can.

Please do not rush through this book! Take the time to mentally process and work through each activity. Each activity takes thought and is aimed at helping you break years of mental and or physical unhealthy habits. This is a journey and not a race! With losing nearly 200 pounds, I can promise you I have had my shares of highs and lowes. With that being said, I still push forward. I know my God has a plan for my life and I need to be in the best of shape! Just as there is a set destiny for my life, I believe the same for your life.

I love you! I wish you much success and happiness!

Your FAB Motivator,

Clarissa Young

Chapter 1 My Breaking point

Often times I am asked, "When did you get to the point that you said enough is enough?" To be honest, I clearly remember the day that I thought, "I have finally had enough." Standing at 515 pounds and basically imprisoned in my own body; seems like I would have been fed up a long time ago. The day that I was at my breaking point was very rough for me. I still remember holding back tears as I was in a public setting and too ashamed to cry. I remember the loneliness I felt. I remember the disappointment I felt. I remember being scared. I remember knowing I wanted better but did not know how it was going to happen. I remember feeling like just do it… Just eat right and loose weight, but I simply could not. I feel like I have been dieting all of my life. With that said, I knew I had a basic knowledge of what I needed to do to lose weight but was lacking the willpower to last long enough to get the job done. I would tell myself, enough is enough; I am going to start my healthy lifestyle on Monday. Monday comes, and by lunchtime, I had eaten something I promised myself that I would not eat. Before I knew it, I was waiting for another Monday to reset again.

So here it goes… My breaking point. It was during the Christmas season, and my oldest son Tyler, my husband Angelo, and I was out celebrating the holidays. At that time, Tyler was 4 years old, and Angelo and I had only been dating for a few months. Let me give you a little background on Tyler and I. Tyler is who I call "my first true love." In life, I felt like I had been searching for love in so many places but only receiving conditional love. Meaning the "love" that would only love you on your good days or when it is convenient for them. No offense to my family or friends because I was surrounded by so many people that showed me love, but still I felt like something was missing. So, I call him "my first true love." Though it was not love at first sight like most mothers with their children. No guys, If I am being 100% honest, it was not love at first sight. I remember when he was first born, and

I saw him for the first time my thoughts were OMG he got a fat nose. LOL. Well, he was 9 pounds and 10 ounces. Everything was fat about my little one. The biggest baby in the NICU.

Within days I grew in love, but then that love was tainted by fear. I feared that I would lose him like I lost other people that I loved. Though I didn't lose them all to death, the relationships were not the best as I would have liked them to be. I'm referring to parents, siblings, ex-boyfriends, etc....; you name it. It just seemed like as soon as I opened my heart, something would go wrong. So, you see when I had my Tyler, my baby, I knew that I had love, I knew that he would love me and I knew that I would love him too. Only death could separate us. So, I began to worry that he was going to die, and I would pray to God not to take my baby away. At the time, I even informed the church I attended of my fears. To be honest, I think I may have been suffering from slight postpartum depression. This kid of mine meant the world to me, for many years some have come and gone, but for the most part, it was him and me. Son and Mommy. Tyler was my everything and my all in all. I was very much so a momma bear when it came to him, and I have always been a very involved mother. We did everything together. We baked, we did arts and crafts, we went to the circus, we went to the movies, we watched tv, we did everything that I could do… Sitting down! In fact, I don't think besides the 10 days after birth where he stayed in the hospital, that we had ever spent a full day apart until he was around 2 years old.

Back to my breaking point. We arrived at the Christmas event; it's a beautiful outside family event that stretches about 2 blocks long. As soon as we pulled up to the event, anxiety begins to kick in as we could not find close parking. The Christmas lights were gleaming and fake Florida snow was in the air. My baby had the biggest joy in his heart, but I was in despair. After parking, we immediately got out of the car and walked over to the event. It took me 5 minutes to arrive at the event, a person in shape could have walked the same distance in 1 minute. I immediately needed to sit down and that's what I did. I sat down and took a long glare down the block with all the festivities. To me, it looked like 3 miles of activities, in all it probably was about a 3rd of a mile stretch. I just could not do it due to the pain. My knees, my back, and my spirit were hurting. I saw the joy in Tyler's face when Angelo told me that he and Tyler will go do a few things and they would be back. I asked Tyler was he sure he wanted to go, and of course, he said yes. I was hurt but truly understood. My baby did not want to sit. He wanted to walk and enjoy the festivities. At this point, I took a flash-forward mental view of Tyler's life. I began to think about how I could lose my baby's love and attention because of my immobility. I began to see him wanting to go places and wanting to do things that I was just not in shape to do. In fact, it was around the age 4 that I started planning him a Birthday Party to Race Car Extreme. Race Car Extreme is a big indoor park that is really nice, well so I think. (I still have not personally gone). There were 2 big problems with planning this birthday party. For one, he had to be eight years old, no biggie, if

2

God is willing, he will turn 8 years old one day. The second was mommy needs to be able to fit in the go-kart. Because of the fear of me not being able to fit in that kart we have yet to go to the facility. I don't know if Tyler even knows it exists. This was just one of many things that I was afraid that I would miss out on if I did not get my health together.

I did not want to miss out on this festival, the go-karts, or any other event in my baby's life because I could not physically stand for over five minutes. As I sat at the Christmas event, it was hot, but I felt cold. Though it was packed with people, I felt alone, as I watched my baby walk hand and hand with my boyfriend at the time. I felt more alone as I watched everyone else laugh, smile, walk, and take pictures with their family. I had no one to take photos with. To be honest, I don't think my confidence was even high enough to want to take a picture. Now don't get me wrong, once they invented the delete button and I could delete all the pictures before anyone else could see, I had no problem taking pictures. I would delete any pictures that I thought my stomach looked too big, my butt looked too flat or anything else that I did not like. LOL. All those pictures with me at my heaviest on social media such were the cream of the crop. You couldn't tell me I was not looking skinny in my pictures. Not this day, I didn't want to take any pictures. I just really wanted to go home. Go home, put my baby to bed, and just cry.

Angelo and Tyler did arrive back with pictures, and because I was not there, I was not in the photos. Therefore, I will not be a part of this memory. As I looked at the pictures, I smiled and appeared to be happy that my baby had a good time and that Angelo was able to save the day. Even though my baby really did look cute in his reindeer antlers, I wanted to be there. I wanted to be a part of the memory, not hear about the memory. I kept up a smile, but on the inside, I was crying.

After we drove home, what seemed like a longer than usual ride was also a quiet ride. I did not say anything, and neither did they. Though we only lived about 5 minutes away. It felt like a 30-minute drive. I did as most moms would do and kept my composure together long enough to put my baby to bed. I remember going to my room alone. As much as I tried to hide it, Angelo was very much aware and this night he stayed out on the couch. Truthfully, I wished I could've been held and that he would've told me that it was going to be ok. In his mind, his way of helping was to give me my space. As much as I really wanted him there, this was the time I needed to spend with God. So, as I went into my room and shut my door, I began to cry. That cry went from tears rolling, to tears rolling with sobbing, to tears running with sobbing and yelling. That was the moment I began to cry out to God for help. I have asked for help from God plenty of times regarding this matter, but this time, I was pleading for my life. I was at a point where if he would not help me, then I'd rather not live. I began to think about who would take care of my baby. No one could love "my first true love," the way I do! I could not leave him, and I was not trying to go to hell by taking him with me. Yes, the thought did cross my mind. I was in a really tough spot. I wasn't terrified of being 515 pounds and dying. I wasn't scared of the morbid conditions that could come from being obese. I was not fearful of how I looked or what others thought of me. I was crying because I was afraid of missing out on what's to come in my baby's life. I was scared of him having memories and me not being in them. I was scared that the one person I loved the most, would live a life that I could not be a part of.

Being overweight can be a very daunting thing, and I know there are so many people that can relate to the pain that I felt. Many times, people think of weight issues, and they think of image or health. Whereas in reality, most of us suffer mentally. It is the feeling of being scared, hopeless, isolated, imprisoned, or depressed. To those people, I would like to say, "you're not alone, and you have found your help in me."

I have written this book to provide you hope, vision, belief, and to start a fight on the inside of you that will not die down. You will help YOU accomplish your goals. This book is to let others know that no matter how down you are, you can get back up. To let others remember that no matter how far your goal may seem it is achievable. To allow others to know that through God, all things are possible. Your goals may not be accomplished overnight, but with you intentionally growing your faith and being persistent eventually your goals will be achieved.

As we get ready to dive deeper into this journey, I do not want you to go at this alone. When trusting God we turn our finances over to him. We turn our relationships over to him. We turn cancer and diseases over to him. Let's also use him when it comes to aspects of losing weight.

Let us pray.

Father God, we come to you today saying, thank you for your life. Thank you for the new day. Thank you for always being there and waiting for us to come to you for help, guidance, and support. At this very moment, we call on you, God. We ask for endurance to read and finish this book. We ask for a clear interpretation. We ask that we can take the information in this book and use it for good in our lives and others around us. We bind up the spirit of defeat, the spirit of depression, the spirit of Isolation, and any other lingering spirits that are not of you, Lord. We ask that you have your way, Lord. We give you full permission to come into our lives and do what is necessary to help us get our health back on track. We shut down any attacks of the enemy that have kept us off our destined path. We ask that you forgive us for anything that we may have personally done that turned us off the path that you have prepared for us. For we know that you knew us before we were in our mother's womb and from day 1, our lives were attached to a specific plan. We pray healing over all our bodies. We pray for mental and physical healing in everyone that comes in contact with the content in this book, whether it be through firsthand or hearsay. We pray that joints are pain-free, we pray that diseases and cancers miraculously disappear. We pray that food addictions and sleep apnea exist no more. Lord, you know our every need, and our heart desires. Have your way, Lord. Have your way. In Jesus mighty name, we pray. Amen

Let's address some "Common barriers to weight loss."

Depression

How to deal with depression? First, it is for you to know at what level you are depressed? Are you depressed to the point where you periodically have sad thoughts or is your everyday life affected? Are you no longer the person spiritually that you used to be?
If you find that you have 6 out of 12 of these conditions, please seek professional help along with reading this book.

Common Symptoms of depression are:
- Anxiety, agitation or restlessness
- Unexplained aches and pains, such as back pain, stomach cramps, or headaches
- Sleep disturbance, early-morning wakefulness or sleeping too much
- Feelings of sadness, guilt, helplessness, tearfulness, emptiness or hopelessness
- Angry outbursts, irritability or frustration, even over small matters
- Loss of interest or pleasure in most or all normal activities, such as sex, hobbies, or sports
- Fatigue, tiredness, and lack of energy to do any activities
- Change in eating habits, reduced appetite/ weight loss or increased cravings for food/ weight gain
- Slowed thinking, speaking or body movements
- Feelings of worthlessness or guilt, fixating on past failures or self-blame
- Trouble thinking, concentrating, making decisions and remembering things
- Persistent or recurrent thoughts of death, suicidal thoughts, suicide attempts or suicide

If you find that while reading these symptoms you experience many of these, it is best to seek professional help along with reading this book. Some signs of depression come with the everyday hustle and bustle; however, it is better to get checked out and know that you are ok, versus facing these conditions alone. Depression is not a sign of being weak or it is not something that you can just simply fix overnight. Many people that suffer from depression can seek relief through medication, psychotherapy, or both. Also, sometimes we feel as Christians, we can not go through phases of despair if we have faith. God gives us people to help when we are in need; we must receive it. We all go through trials and tribulations. Sometimes intervention is needed. Always resort to your faith base first. Pray that God sends help that lines up with your values and beliefs. Pray that all information is giving with a retrospective to your faith. Pray that you receive what was ordained for you to receive.

FAB Activity #1/ Overcoming feelings of being sad:

Often when overweight, some also find themselves unhappy about the situation. Though we are not all depressed, some of us may suffer from feelings of being sad. Here are some ideas of things to do to help lift your spirits.

1. Write- Writing can be a great form of venting. It allows you to really address how you feel and to release those feelings correctly. Examples would be to simply journal, write poetry, or write stories. Even better, write affirmation turning your negative sad feelings into positive happy feelings.

2. Be of help- Sometimes when we help others, in return it helps us feel valuable and makes us feel needed. Examples of how you can help: Wait to hold the door open for someone walking from afar, offer to help an elderly put groceries into a car, give flowers to a random person and wish them a great day, volunteer at a hospital or food bank. I can remember the time I purchased 5 plants, and I walked around the local shopping plaza and passed them out to random women. The women that did not think I was crazy, happily accepted them. LOL. The smile on their faces was priceless, and I am sure that they in return went and did a good favor for someone else that day.

3. Exercise- Get the body moving!!! When we exercise, we release endorphins that help us feel better within or chemical makeup. Examples: Take a 10-minute walk, go window shopping, clean your home, dance to your favorite song (make sure that the song is spiritually uplifting). Many times, when we are sad we listen to sad music making the matter worse. No need to listen to a song with a woman talking about her man cheating when you are already not in a good mood; that song will not help.

Bible verses to meditate on that will further help with this topic:
- You, Lord, are my lamp; the Lord turns my darkness into light. **2 Samuel 22:29**
- "Come to me, all you who are weary and burden, and I will give you rest. Take my yoke upon you and learn from me, for I am gentle and humble in heart, and you will find rest for your souls. For my yoke is easy, and my burden is light." **Matthew 11:28-30**

Another common barrier to weight loss is fear

Fear

Many people are afraid, and I was too. Afraid to start, scared to fail, scared because I didn't know what to do. Scared to reach out to others for help. Fear is a plot of the enemy. Many times in life, we are afraid of things that do not even exist.

Definition of scared- thrown into or being in a state of fear, fright or panic.

FAB Activity #2/ Getting Rid of fear:

1. Do not overthink your journey. It is ok to crawl before you walk. Many times, people jump into a diet program and want to go cold turkey, causing them to feel deprived and eventually quit. A scenario is a person that has been eating meat all their lives. They love meat, and today they decided they are no longer going to eat meat again. Now some people do have this willpower, but many of us have to develop these habits. It is better to make small cuts, adapt, than make small cuts again.

2. Make realistic goals. Goals should be fully mapped out with a clear objective, they should state "how to" and have time frames. Goals should be task-oriented and not goal-oriented. Meaning, focus on what you need to do to obtain your goal. You can stare at a penny on the ground for hours and wish it was heads up. If you only wish for it to be heads up, but not take action, it remains there on the ground tails down!

Bad Goal Example: My Goal is to lose 20 pounds in 4 months.

Good Goal Example: My goal is to drink 60oz of water every day. My goal is to exercise 3 days a week for 1 hour at a time. My goal is to monitor my food and keep carbs under 100 grams every day. In achieving these short-term goals for 4 months, my long-term goal is to lose 20 pounds.

To be without hope is another common weight loss barrier

Feeling Hopeless

Many times, people feel hopeless. Have you ever tried to diet and it seemed like you did everything right, but would not see the pounds on the scale go down? Or have you dieted to lose 5 pounds, but the next week even though it seems like you dieted the very same way you end up gaining the 5 pounds back and maybe more? I totally have been there before, but I promise you that you can do this and that there is hope.

Hope is very much a mental thing. You must believe that you can do something to accomplish it. I challenge you first to visualize yourself accomplishing your goals. Let's look a little deeper into the goal. Let's be honest, most of us could care less what the number on the scale says if we liked how we looked and felt. An example would be if the scale could say you are

250 pounds, but if you looked like you weighed 170 pounds and was limber and filled with so much energy, you probably would not be upset. So, let's vision us in beautiful dresses. Let's picture ourselves with less stomach pudge. Let's view our self in the best shape ever. You can do all the desires of your heart because you have great endurance, you are pain-free, and your self-esteem is through the roof. Whether you believe this or not I am speaking positivity over your life. All obtained dreams started with a vision. For you to be healthy, it begins with you seeing yourself healthy.

FAB Activity #3/ Visualizing your goals:
Draw and/or write out a thorough description of yourself **at your goal weight.**
1. How do you feel at your goal weight (Happy, Energetic, Adventurous)?
2. What do you like to wear at your goal weight? (What color, what material, what length and fit)
3. How do others see you? (Happy, beautiful, secure)
4. What activities will you do at your goal weight? (Ice Skate, Zip Line, write a book)
5. What are some things that you will get rid of or stop doing at your goal weight? (People, food, clothing, thoughts)

Another common barrier to losing weight is Isolation:
Isolation

For many people being overweight can also cause isolation. I remember being surrounded by family, but still was feeling alone. I was not able to share a lot of my deep hidden pain. I felt that most people thought "if you want to lose weight… just do it," so they would not understand. I was also the one that everyone thought had such high self-esteem and a beautiful smile. How could I share that I was hurting and that I often felt like killing myself? Then, there is the physical isolation. Not being able to go to certain events because you could not walk too far or stand too long. Not going because of the anxiety, wondering if they had chairs, do the chairs have arms, are the chair legs sturdy enough, and what will others think of me? Not being able to find the proper clothing or shoes to fit the event. I could go on and on about isolation, but I want to look at the positive. YOU ARE NOT ALONE! With God, you can do this thing. God will put people in your life to help you through all situations.

In life, God sends people called destiny helpers. Many times, we receive help, but because it was not in the form that we asked, we may not recognize it as help. Let's use an example of being low on money. Have you ever had someone help you with money? I'm sure some of you reading this may have answered no... but let's look more into the matter. Maybe you were low on cash and did not have enough gas in your car to last you the rest of the week. Randomly a friend asks you for a ride and in return gives you gas. Not only does that gas get you to their location, but it is also enough for you to get to work for the rest of the week. Let's look at another example, you have a job in your home that needs immediate attention like a pipe burst. At this time, you do not have a lot of money, but a friend refers you to a friend. This friend not only does a great job at the repair but also gives you a discount because you are associated with their friend. Yes, you had to spend money, but because of God, you were linked with a friend, who knew a friend that was certified to do the job, who in return offered you a discount. I encourage you to think positive about your interactions with people and to pray that God sends positive people in your life to bring growth and not harm. I pray that you are able to open-heartedly perceive your blessings and not be a hindrance to your own destiny.

FAB Activity #4/ Building a Support System:

Intentionally build relationships and surround yourself with positive people. Write down 3 people that you can talk to or go if you feel down.

Examples: Church, Family, Friends, Neighbors, Social Media Page, Social Media Group,

Possible people to build a relationship with

1.
2.
3.

After creating your list, be sure also to write their name and number. (If they accept this responsibility, they will be your emergency contact list) Beforehand, you are to call them and let them know that you value them and you would like to use them for your emergency support system. Let them know that sometimes in life, things can be tough, and we need a friend that we can count on. Then agree not to misuse this emergency contact. If they agree to be your emergency support person, then create a code word with them. Write your code word down. Let them promise if you call or text, and you mention the code word that they will immediately respond to you. Pick 3 people. Keep in mind that everyone may not be available on demand. So, don't feel upset, prepare ahead of time by having two alternative people. 1 out of 3 should be available. You must also promise only to use this code word in an emergency situation. You do not want to be like the little boy who called wolf, and no one responds when you really need them. Set clear boundaries on what is an emergency versus a time that you simply need to vent.

Another common barrier that comes with being overweight is imprisonment.

Imprisonment

Many times, imprisonment and isolation can feel very similar. I believe imprisonment is when you have the ability to do something, but not freedom. You have the time, you have the money, you have the support, but you just can't do it. As I type, I think of a memory with some of my friends on a boat trip. It was so much fun when it was all over, and as I reflect back the entire experience was not fun. I had to break the fear of being able to climb on the boat. I pushed that fear aside and climbed on the boat. We arrived at our destination, and I start to feel anxious about being able to do the planned activities. I'll never forget the trampoline on the side of the boat; very daunting. Everyone was jumping off the boat unto the trampoline, 1, 2, 3, 5 at a time. But not I… I was so afraid.

I thought that if I would jump on the trampoline it would move or something worse would happen like it would cave in. Now at this point, I was about 120 pounds lighter than my highest weight of 515 pounds. I was exercising on a regular. Though I was physically prepared, with 5 adult women on the trampoline, I thought to myself how it could hold little old me by myself. I was at a mental standstill. I was encaged in my fear. I stood at the door of the boat looking to jump onto that trampoline for at least 10 minutes. I stood there and simply could not jump. My friends were there the whole time cheering me on… (Especially Natalie… LOL she is always daring me to do something and I love her for it!) Jump, Jump, Jump... You can do it… they yelled. My heart was pounding, my feet felt so heavy, anxiety was in full-blown effect, adrenaline rushing... LOL. After what seemed like an eternity pressure and I was in flight or fight, I JUMPED!!! It was amazing! The trampoline did not break! I did not hurt myself and I was enjoying life.

Too well, this reminds me of the stories of elephants. How, when they are little they are chained at the ankle to stay in one spot. Once they are grown, 1 of 2 things could happen. The chains are removed, and they have the ability to roam free, or they are continued to be chained. Now, for those that are chained as an adult elephant have great strength and can break loose. Both of these elephants chained or unchained because of mental imprisonment they will not roam free. I challenge you to break all mental chains and roam free!

Bible verses to meditate on that will further help with this topic:

- He brought them out of darkness, the utter darkness. And broke away their chains. **Psalms 107:14**
- Don't be afraid I have redeemed you. I have called you by name, and you are mine. **Isaiah 43:1**

FAB Activity #5/ Free yourself from imprisonment:

I challenge you to create a bucket list (Minimum of 3) of things that you desire to do at this very moment, things that you have the ability to do. You have the strength, money, and time, but you are simply scared. Now because you are scared on first thought, you may not believe that you have the ability to complete the task. So, I really want you to think hard about what is the worst that could happen if you try and fail, then on the same hand think about how great you would feel that you accomplished this... Is it worth the risk? Maybe you want to do a sexy private photoshoot, perhaps you go jet skiing (LOL I'm working on the courage for this one), maybe you take a special trip and just have fun!!!

<u>Bucket List</u>

1.
2.
3.
4.
5.
6.

7.
8.
9.
10.

Chapter 2 Love Yourself

Once you hit your breaking point, the hardest thing to do at times is to simply love yourself. Often, we want to find the perfect diet or the perfect product, but in reality, if you do not love yourself, then almost all plans will fail. I often reflect on when I weighed 515 pounds. Many people thought I had high self-esteem. I believed for others to think I was pretty that I needed to act like I thought I was pretty. I would dress nice, hold my head high, but deep down inside I was not happy with the quality of my life. I will be honest, my "self-love" did not happen overnight. Yes, losing some weight has helped with my self-esteem. However, I am in love with the change in the quality of my life more so than the number on the scale.

When I injured my leg in February 2019, it helped me to realize this. I was 170 pounds lighter at the time of my injury, but back with limited mobility. So, the numbers on the scale were better, but I was in pain every step I took. During these days in pain, I was torn. Many days, I wanted to get up and be active, but I was in pain. I had gotten used to being able to move with little discomfort. I had to love myself enough to know that I deserve to fight for the things I wanted in life. I knew that life was not over, but I simply had to modify it to fit my current situation. Here are some modifications that you can make today to grow to love yourself tomorrow.

Using Affirmations to improve self-love

Affirmations: *the action or process of affirming something or being affirmed.*

Affirmations are when you begin to speak into your life. Your mind only knows what you tell it. We say affirmations all the time; unfortunately, a lot of times the affirmations we use are negative. "I will never get this weight off me." "I don't like to exercise." "I love to eat junk food." Does any of this sound familiar? For many of us, I'm sure we say it or at least know someone who says it. The great thing about our mind is that it is reprogrammable; I know this firsthand. I was once the type of person that was too ashamed to take pictures, I would not wear sleeveless clothes, and I refused to look into a full-body mirror. I continue to work on myself every day, but I am way past where I used to be mentally. We can change what we think of ourselves. Rather if we feel this way because of our own thoughts or because of what someone else said, let's use our affirmations for positive speaking into our lives.

So how to create winning affirmations? Make sure all your affirmations are positive. Make sure all your affirmation speaks into the present. Say your affirmations out loud and with confidence. It is ok if we do not currently believe our affirmation. However, I do need you to believe that one day by the grace of God, you will be able to walk in your affirmations. You must have hope and vision that what you are saying, even if you do not know how or when it is going to occur.
Here are some of my affirmations for example.

I am so happy that my health is better than ever, that my knees are pain-free and that I am enjoying physical activity. (Even during my knee injury, I was speaking this into my life)

I am so grateful that I am in control of what I eat. I love to eat healthy and I eat carbs in moderation.

I am so blessed that I now make $5,000 a month. I am thrilled that all my bills are paid, that I am saving money, and that I have enough money to help others. (Again, at this moment $5K is not tangible, but it is believable)

FAB Activity #6/ Creating Positive life-changing affirmations:
Start by thinking about what is going on in your life. What are some things that you want to change? Your change can be from bad to good, or from good to better. All things in life should show growth. There is nothing wrong with having, being grateful, and aligning yourself for greater.

Write down the things that you would like to change. Use positive affirmations to speak on the change.   Create 3 positive affirmations. Say them at least 3 times a day for at least 4 weeks or until you see them come to the past. Say them out loud, be bold, smile, maybe even try looking into a mirror while saying them.

Sometimes it is great to look at ourselves in the mirror because it will show us how others see us. Have you ever had someone ask you what's wrong; and you thought everything was ok? Even though your words say one thing, your facial expressions and body language can say another. All of these need to line up. Your face, words, and body language need to ooze positivity into your life.

1.	
2.	
3.	

Bible verses to meditate on that will further help with this topic:

- Christ has set me free to experience true freedom. **Galatians 5:1**
- God is my refuge, strength, and help in times of trouble. **Psalm 46:1**
- Because I believe in Jesus, I no longer live in darkness. **John 13:46**
- I choose to have the same attitude that Jesus had. **Philippians 2:5**

Look good to feel good

Posture

I'm a firm believer in when you look good, you feel good. When you feel good, you do good! What is something you can do today to make yourself feel better? Maybe slap on some lipstick? put your favorite outfit on or do something special to your hair? Whatever makes you feel good, do it, and do it often. While you're doing it be aware of your body language. I know someone is saying, what does this have to do with losing weight? It has everything to do with it. Until you believe in yourself and have unconditional love for yourself the process of losing weight will be difficult and possibly a dreaded experience. I don't want you to lose weight then learn how to love yourself; you need to love yourself now than losing the weight will come simultaneously. When you love yourself, the journey of reaching your goals is not as daunting, but instead, it is a journey to paradise. Imagine this, you're in a car going out of town and you like the car that you are driving. Doesn't it make the trip more enduring? You enjoy the actual trip, and you are not just hurrying up to get to your destination. When you are in a vehicle that you don't like, for whatever reason, sometimes you miss out on scenic landmarks because you are in such a rush to simply get out of the current environment. You have some people that are sometimes so in a hurry that you even drive reckless and do things that are not safe along the way. Your weight loss journey is the same. If you love yourself when you first start your fitness your journey, you can appreciate and correctly see out the journey to your end goals. If you love yourself, it's more likely that you will be equipped to make a change for the better versus being saddened or depressed by the journey.

Now, back to body language, it says a lot about a person as well as to others and to yourself. Let's take a moment to reflect. When you think of a depressed person how is their posture? Maybe head is down, shoulders are drooping forward, the face frowns... etc. All of these things send messages to your brain. So be sure to set your tone intentionally. Hold your head high, shoulders back, and smile. Deliberately check your posture throughout your day. Make sure that your body language is sending the correct message to others and more importantly to yourself.

FAB Activity #7/ Just Smile

Smile on purpose. Many times, I've read how people who smile live longer and are depressed less. I want you to think of your favorite thing and smile. Examine how you feel. Examine your body posture. I want you to think of something in which you're not as happy with. Examine your body posture. Now I want you to smile, showing all teeth, head high, and shoulders back for 60 Seconds. How do you feel? I'm sure even though you just thought about something that you were not happy about, doing this smiling exercise made you feel better. I want to encourage you to smile on purpose. Smile when you want to cry and smile when you're bored. Smile so much that your smile becomes contagious, and others around you start to smile too!

Bible verses to meditate on that will further help with this topic:
- Cast all of your anxiety on him because he cares for you. **Peter 5:7**
- Let us then approach the throne of grace with confidence, so that we may receive mercy and find grace to help us in our time of need. **Hebrews 4:16**
- He who refreshes others will himself be refreshed. **Proverbs 11:25**
- Rejoice always, pray without ceasing, give thanks in all circumstances; for this is the will of God in Christ Jesus for you. **1 Thessalonians 5:16-18**

To change or not to change???

In this session, we are going to do things a little backward. I want you to do the activity, then we will discuss it. Now that we are feeling good, looking good, and thinking good let's write a list. Imagine that you have a magic wand; you can change anything about your life. What would you change? I want you to write a list of everything you would change. At this point, throw all doubts, throw all how to's, and throw all the what if's out the door. Write as little or as much as you want. I really want you to take this time to reflect on life and the changes that you want to incorporate. This is a critical assignment for your weight loss goals. (Do not skip ahead)

Things I would change about me mentally, spiritually, or physically.

Now that we have this list let's organize it. Put a 1 next to everything that with a little effort you can change. Put a 2 next to everything that you want to change, you can change, but you don't know where to start, how to start, or you have a hard time being consistent after you start.

Lastly, put a 3 next to everything that no matter what happens in life you cannot change. Also remembering that it will be somethings that you cannot change, but God can. If it is something in life that you cannot change, but God can do not place it as a 3, place it as a 2.

Let's first work with all the 3's because you cannot change them. They may have you feeling down, depressed, or hopeless; however, let me first say that you are FABtastic with all imperfections. No matter how jacked up it is, things are the way they are or happen for a reason. You are made with a purpose and you are loved. Deep down inside, we have to learn to love the thing that we hate about ourselves. Example: You have a scar on your face, and it seems that people are always staring. Acceptance is the key. You have a scar, you can conceal and hide it, but at the end of the day, there is still a scar. Accept the scar! Maybe have an artist create you a special painting that beautifies your scar, so when you look at it you don't see the pain and hurt, but you see beauty and art. Let's think of the emotional area... maybe a loved one died. You cannot bring them back. You can hide your sorrow and keep the pain inside, or you can accept it, and celebrate their life. Create a memory. Maybe plant a tree in remembrance of the loved one. Do what make you feel good. This will help you cope with this hurt versus masking it.

Now let's look at all of your 2's. For each of your 2's, I need you to write down why! Why do you want this to happen? How would you feel about the change? What would you accomplish? What changes will be made and what sacrifices will you have to do?

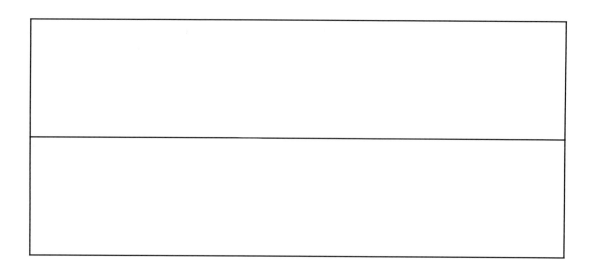

Let's individually look over each why, how you will feel with each goal, and what you will have to sacrifice for each goal. Is it worth the energy that you have to give? Do you really want this thing? If your answer is no, simply cross it off your list and let it be. Maybe, it's a no for now, but can later be worked on. Either way, cross it out and let it be. If your answer is yes. It is time for us to get to work. This will take planning. We are going to focus on the task that needs to get done in order to start this goal. Let's get started right away! Why wait? How bad do you really want it?

Now that we are ready to accomplish our goals, let me explain what I mean by focusing on the task and not on the goal. Let's use getting a bachelor's degree as a goal. There are degree outlines that list all of the classes that you must take before obtaining your degree... your overall goal. You will not check with your Guidance Counselor on a daily basis to ask if you have your bachelors. You will not watch the scale daily to ask did you hit your goal. Within each individual degree, you will have a timeline of specific classes to take at particular times. You must attempt to stay on track and attend all your scheduled classes. You must try to exercise and eat healthy every day. With these classes, some have a prerequisite. Meaning you have to take one course before you can take a particular class. If you have not exercised in years, you should not sign up for a 5K.

Maybe you may need to first master being able to walk 1 mile. Jumping into a class without the pre-knowledge is increasing the risk of you failing. It is also essential to stay consistent with what you are doing. If week 1 your major is Biology, week 2 your major is Geometry, and week 3 your major is Business, you will have a lot of classes. However, you will never obtain a degree. If this week you are doing a low carb diet and you hit a bump and change to something else, then you hit another bump and change to something else; will you ever find what really works? Probably not! Life comes with bumps, turns, and detours, but your destination must remain the same to arrive. This is the same as your journey. Don't be too quick to say something is not working, don't be all or nothing. REMAIN POSITIVE!!! You are going to have to Whoop Whoop through this thing (shout out to my friend Curtis for helping me create this acronym (I will speak more about what Whoop Whop is in Chapter 7)).

W- Willpower- Strong determination that allows you to do something difficult
H-Hope- A desire for a sure thing to happen
O- Optimistic- Confident about the future
O-Oath- A Promise
P-Perseverance- Persistence in doing something despite difficulty

Every time you start your journey and things get challenging remember that "It's FAB when you WHOOP." In life, it's all about Finding your Acceptable Balance. Finding what works for you. Understanding that what works for someone else may not work the same for you. My favorite quote to say when I'm exercising is "modify the modify." Create your way of getting it done. If somethings are in the most basic form, you can always break it down or switch it up more to make it your own. It is only rare occasions in life that you simply cannot do something. YOU CAN DO ALL THINGS!!! You may have to revamp it to fit your needs and ability. When you achieve something that pushed you pass your comfort zone, when you do what others said you couldn't… my friend that's when you are Whoop Whooping!

Lastly, go back to the list. Take all the things that you put a 1 next to and organize them in priority. Starting with number 1 as the most important thing for you to get done. Number 2 as the second and so on... In life, we have been taught to be a multitasker. My friend, in some cases this is the wrong way. Many times, we try to do 100 things at one time and go through life half tailing so much. Focus on 1 maybe 2 goals at a time. Master it, achieve it, then move onto the next. Studies have shown that our brain does not process multitasking that well. That's why we are driving, texting, and crashing. That's why we are cooking, cleaning, and setting off the smoke detectors. Lol. The more hands-on you are with a goal, the faster you can get it down. The quicker you get it done (with focus and precision), the more likely you are to complete the goal.

So, all through life you are going to find that you have things that you want to change about yourself. If you have nothing that you want to change about yourself, then that itself needs to change. Now, I am not saying that you want to be like someone else, but you should always want to be your best you. Everything in life grows, and changes. Look at the flowers, they start as seeds and grow into beautiful flowers.

Even once the flowers bloom, they continue to get more petals, or the leaves themselves begin to change and become more complex. Look at animals as another example, no animal at birth looks or moves the same way once they are an adult. We all are supposed to change and grow into our full purpose in life.

Unfortunately, if your current talent allows you to effortless stay above ground, then more than likely it is not your sole purpose in life. Growth requires stretch, but God wants to make a testimony out of you. If you are a master at your skill, without God's help… How does he get the glory? Your destiny will challenge you!

So, as we are transforming into this great person that God has called us to be, we will find that we have some things that we know how to change and just need to do it. There are also going to be somethings that we want to change but have no clue how to do it. Lastly, we will also have somethings that are stuck like glue. It is what it is. There is no changing it. Let's use the Serenity Prayer to help us with that!

Serenity Prayer
- Reinhold Niebuhr (1892-1971)

God grant me the serenity
to accept the things, I cannot change;
courage to change the things I can;
and wisdom to know the difference.

Living one day at a time;
enjoying one moment at a time;
accepting hardships as the pathway to peace;
taking, as He did, this sinful world
as it is, not as I would have it;
trusting that He will make all things right
if I surrender to His Will;
that I may be reasonably happy in this life
and supremely happy with Him

forever in the next.

Amen.

To love yourself is to prepare yourself for everything that is to come on this journey...

I am my priority

This journey is a lifestyle change. In the beginning you're going to have to learn to be selfish. On one hand, you're going to love some people and somethings. On the other hand, you are going to have to let some people and some things go. Now some of these things you may be able to pick back up later... and some of these things you may learn that you are better off without. When you first start your journey or when you are re-starting your weight loss journey temptation will be all around. For example; have you ever planned your diet out? I mean you took the time to make a meal schedule. You took the time to go grocery shopping. You took the time to cook the food. You have your exercise plan. You have your list of to do's and not to do's. You are ready to start on Saturday. Lol. I know some are saying I would never start on a Saturday... Lol, that's a stall in itself that we will talk about later in this book. You don't need a Monday, a 1st of the month, a New Year, or anything else to jump right in. Back to you starting on Saturday, you are set and ready to start tomorrow... Saturday! You've prepared for the last 4 days, then your friend calls... She says, Girl what you are doing tomorrow???... "Saturday" "I really wanted you toooooo.... with me". Nine times out of ten, she is not calling for you to help her start her new diet. It's either to go to a party, go for a drink, go out to eat, or something that will tempt you to step aside from your schedule. If you are not careful all of the planning that you did over the last 3 days can be overthrown by partying with your friend, and if you are like most of us you probably gained a few pounds while waiting for Saturday.   Since these were your last "free days" and come Saturday, you mean "business" you had to let yourself splurge or workout less. So, at this point, you have 2 options. You can tell your friend I'm super sorry, but I can't make it... Talking about now feeling isolated or you can "Start" on Monday... Sounds familiar?? I guess there is also a 3rd option. That is to go ahead with your friend but be very disciplined and not do anything outside of what you have taken the time to plan. The only issue with that is most of us are not disciplined enough to stick to the plan. So, it's time to learn how to prepare in advance. Let's be realistic, this is a lifestyle change. Things are going to come up. It is better to prepare for the unexpected versus to say that you are not going to engage with people and events any longer until you reach your goal.

FAB Activity #8/Preparation before the invite:

1. Write down your "why???"… Keep this somewhere as a reminder of why you are making these changes and sacrifices. (Maybe take a picture and keep it with you in your phone)

<table>
<tr><td></td></tr>
<tr><td></td></tr>
<tr><td></td></tr>
<tr><td></td></tr>
<tr><td></td></tr>
<tr><td></td></tr>
<tr><td></td></tr>
</table>

2. What are your limitations? Maybe you can have diet soda. Perhaps you can have half slice of cake with no icing. What are your weaknesses? You may have to rethink these before the event as well as making sure you don't leave out anything. Try to stick to your list as much as possible.

3. Bring your own snacks to events. Many times, if you choose to not eat it causes attention, or it gives you more temptation. While others are eating, bring a healthy snack that you really enjoy. It would be kind of hard to snack on raw broccoli while others are eating ribs. Unless you just loveeee you some broccoli. List a few of your favorite healthy snacks.

4. Make your own plate. Often times, when you go to a party or a gathering people get very heavy-handed with food, especially the starches and things that bulk us up. Things like rice, pasta, etc. If you cannot make your own plate, then ask for an empty plate. Many of us were raised to "finish your plate" Meaning, eat all the food on your plate; stuffed or not. So even if you are full, you continued to eat. With the empty plate, you are to put food up for later. This will help you control portion sizes. Also, if you are the type of person that eats past being full, eat what you like the most first. If you save the best for last, you are more likely to overeat. Now, if you are the type to stop as soon as you feel full in your case it is best to eat the healthiest food first. Your Fiber, your protein, that way once you get to the carbs you are more likely to be already full and not want to eat them. Also, remember all carbs are not bad. We need complex carbs… "Knowing your carbs" will also later be addressed.

5. Opt for water. Choose water for many different reasons. For one it's zero calories. I personally rather eat my calories than drink them. A glass or 2 of soda/pop will give you many extra calories and sugar before you even notice it. Soda also dehydrates you and can make you overeat. Frequently, we confuse the signal of being thirsty for hunger. We then eat food, but really our body was asking for water. Now, being that we still didn't give water, it appears that we are never full because we continue to get this thirsty signal that we are misinterpreting. Also, water is a filler. So, if your full-on water you are less likely to overeat. Lastly, if others are drinking and you are empty-handed, it goes back to you standing out, and you may even possibly feel left out. Sipping on a glass of water while others sip on their drink keeps you on track with your goals. Hey, you can even be extra fancy and add lemon to your water. Lol

At the end of the day, you will decide to attend this event or to simply sit this one out. As I started to walk more into my Christian life, I learned it was many things that I enjoyed doing that I had to say no to. That's not to say that Christians don't do these particular things, but to say I was not ready for it. Example: I love music, and I love to dance. Which is not a problem. Dancing and listening to music will not get you crucified. However, as a baby in

Christ, I had to limit some events cause when I dance and listen to music I also like to have a drink. For some Christians, having a drink is also not a problem (to each his own) However, my goal at that time was not to simply have a drink, but to get as drunk as possible. To be inebriated is to sin.

Bible verses to meditate on that will further help with this topic:
- Do not get drunk on wine, which leads to debauchery. Instead, be filled with the Spirit, **Ephesians 5:18**
- Wine is a mocker and beer a brawler; whoever is led astray by them are not wise. **Proverbs 20:1**
- Let us behave decently, as in daytime, not in carousing and drunkenness, not in sexual immorality and debauchery, not in dissension and jealousy. **Romans 13:13**

Debauchery- Extreme indulgence in bodily pleasures. Crazy partying and wild nights usually accompanied by a lot of alcohol. (*Merriam-Webster*)

Not to say that I am sin-free, but this is one temptation I can now avoid. However, until my flesh was strong enough to listen to music and not correlate the habit of getting drunk, I had to limit my music and environments. I think this is what really grew my love for Zumba. I was able to party and dance while working on my fitness and not feel personally condemned at the same time. At the beginning of my Christian journey, I had to say no to some parties. I had to say no to hanging with some people. This helped me decrease the temptation of me going against my goals of growing stronger with Christ. Now, that I am a little stronger I find that there are still some events that though I am stronger, I know I still don't belong. So while your goal may be to lose weight or be more active you may find that it will be certain people or activities that may not hurt your goals, but it may tempt you to do something that does not help your purpose. So, in the end, we have to decide what is most important.

Bible verses to meditate on that will further help with this topic:
- As a dog returns to its vomit, so fools repeat their folly. **Proverbs 26:11**

- So get rid of your old self, which made you live as you used to—the old self that was being destroyed by its deceitful desires. Your hearts and minds must be made completely new, and you must put on the new self, which is created in God's likeness and reveals itself in the true life that is upright and holy.
No more lying, then! Each of you must tell the truth to the other believer because we are all members together in the body of Christ. If you become angry, do not let your anger lead you into sin, and do not stay angry all day. Don't give the Devil a chance. If you used to rob, you must stop robbing and start working, in order to earn an honest living for yourself and to be able to help the poor. Do not use harmful words,

but only helpful words, the kind that builds up and provides what is needed, so that what you say will do good to those who hear you. And do not make God's Holy Spirit sad; for the Spirit is God's mark of ownership on you, a guarantee that the day will come when God will set you free. Get rid of all bitterness, passion, and anger. No more shouting or insults, no more hateful feelings of any sort. Instead, be kind and tender-hearted to one another, and forgive one another, as God has forgiven you through Christ. **Ephesians 4: 22-32**

- I appeal to you, my friends, as strangers and refugees in this world! Do not give in to bodily passions, which are always at war against the soul. **1 Peter 2:11**

What is love?

Getting the right love from the right person

Often times, when we think of giving love we always expect to receive it back. We can love ourselves all day, but it feels nice when others love us. The thing is that many people feel unloved or unsupported when through their fitness journey. Let me first start by saying, this is YOUR fitness journey. So, you must get it done no matter if you have help, love, validation, or anything else from others. Often times, we have support and love, but we are asking for the wrong things from the right person. Let's take this, for example, a husband and a wife scenario. The husband wants to help the wife eat right. His way of helping is to point out the things that she eats wrong. This, in the end, makes her feel bad and judged. If the two were to communicate on exactly how she receives help, it could be accepted as help/love vs. criticism. He could do something as help her meal prep, buy healthy snacks, and give compliments when she is eating right which will encourage the behavior. Yes, we do these things with our kids, but validation through praise and rewards works great with adults too. Let us look at this from another angle. You are on your fitness journey.

You have a friend who you believe needs to lose weight, and she also agreed that she knows that she wants to lose weight. However, she battles with arthritis, and she is in a lot of pain when she exercises. However, you guys together create a workout routine. At the time of creation, it sounds useful to both of you. Now, it's time to put it in action and your friend is MIA. She is missing in action. More than likely, she didn't flake on you because she doesn't love you, or because she doesn't want to support you. Nine times out of ten, she is mentally struggling with this exercise plan for several reasons. Unfortunately, physical pain can cause mental and spiritual setbacks.

For this reason, this friend may not be a good fit for a "workout" accountability partner. However, this friend has been eating clean for the last 6 months. She knows so much about calories in vs. calories out, and she is very disciplined in what she eats. If you were to link with this friend on her strength vs. linking on your shared weaknesses, she would be a much better accountability partner for you. Often times, when searching for an accountability partner we seek those who we feel comfortable with. Those who are on the same level as us.

A great accountability partner is one that can genuinely help hold you accountable. If neither one of you enjoys exercising, and neither one of you are adamant about working out, who is holding who accountable?

FAB Activity #9/ Accountability Partner:

Let's write down a list of people we are close to, whether in person or on social media. Don't focus on your needs when writing your list. Just write people. Maybe 5 to 10 people that you feel close to.

1
2
3
4
5
6
7

8
9
10

Now that you have them listed, go back and record their strengths. What are they good at? What do they enjoy doing? Think about how does that enjoyment benefits you??? Yes, your friend's happiness and strength can help you if you use it the right way! Example: You love to dance and your next-door neighbor loves to dance. She or he is very good at it too. Dancing is exercise. They would be a great accountability partner.

Using the list above, pick 3 accountability partners. What can they help you with?

1
2
3

Hang tight before reaching out to them! In chapter 5 you will learn how to get the best support from your accountability partner.

Bible verses to meditate on that will further help with this topic:
- But God also created Adam with a need for help from another person. He created Eve with this purpose in mind: "it is not good for man to be alone; I will make him a helper suitable for him" **Genesis 2:18**
- "Bear one another burdens and so fulfill the law of Christ" **Galatians 6:2**
- Let us, therefore, come boldly to the throne of grace, that we may obtain mercy and find grace to help in time of need. **Hebrews 4:16**

- Ask and it will be given to you; seek, and you will find; knock, and it will be opened to you. **Matthew 7:7**

It's A Party

It's a party, and you are the star. Set your small short-term goals and make sure you celebrate yourself each step along the way. Often times when we do things, we say that's part of being an adult or getting things done. With this attitude, we rarely reward ourselves. Rewarding ourselves is very important. It makes you feel good, and when you feel good, you are more likely to keep going. Don't wait to accomplish your long-term goal to love on and celebrate yourself. Love and celebrate your journey as you go. You just started or re-started your journey, and you said that you were going to work out 3 days a week. At the end of the week, you did not lose any weight, and you may have even gained a pound. A pound of muscle (the scale does not know the difference). However, you set a goal to work out 3 times this week, and you did precisely that... You deserve a reward. Actually, you probably need an award, especially if you didn't go down on the scale like you intended to.

How to pick rewards? Rewards should be something that you personally like having or like doing. Rewards should not go against your long-term goal. Let's say your goal is to lose 50 pounds. You exercised your 3 days this week. Going out for dinner may not be the best reward, especially if we eat things that are not in alignment with our goals. It is my personal recommendation to take food totally out of the reward box. These days in time we eat for everything. We eat when we are happy, sad, and in between.

Your reward should also match your accomplishments. If you exercised 3 days a week and you reward yourself with a pedicure when you do something such as hit a 20 pounds weight loss goal, then you have to go all out. Lol. Maybe you regularly get a pedicure, but this time you put a design on every toe. Be extra because you deserve it! Now with that being said, make rewards realistic. We are setting our awards in advance. Don't set yourself up for disappointment. Example: Your reward for exercising 3 days is to go to the movies on the weekend. However, you work all weekend and will not have time to do so. Your rewards must be available to you when it comes to time, finances, obtainability, etc.

Please remember to focus on task-related goals vs. scale goals. Focus on things that you can do to achieve your goal versus the actual target. Meaning instead of focusing on scale, inches, getting into a dress, or running a 5K. Focus on the steps that you must take daily to build up to those goals. Most importantly love yourself throughout the process.

FAB Activity #10/ Rewarding you:

List possible rewards for yourself. List things that you like or enjoy doing. We will create goals and match rewards at a later time. For now, simply think of awards.

Rewards

1	
2	
3	
4	
5	
6	
7	
8	
9	

10

Bible verses to meditate on that will further help with this topic:

- And now these three remain: faith, hope, and love. But the greatest of these is love. **1 Corinthians 13:13**
- Don't let anyone look down on you because you are young, but set an example for the believers in speech, in conduct, in love, in faith, and in purity. **1 Timothy 4:12**
- None of us ever hate our own bodies. Instead, we feed them, and take care of them, just as Christ does the church; **Ephesians 5:29**
- You're beautiful from head to toe, my dear love, beautiful beyond compare, absolutely flawless. **Song of Songs 4:7**

Chapter 3 What to do?

OK. You are excited, you are feeling loved, you are ready to reward yourself... now, what??? Now the work beginssss. In this chapter, I want to pose a question. Do you really not know what to do? Take a moment to reflect.

I   n most cases, if we answer honestly, we know what to do, but it's merely a matter of doing it. I know for some of us, this may be an offensive statement. To indeed lose weight, we must be 100% honest with ourselves and really address some of our mental limitations. If you tell yourself you don't know what to do to lose weight, likely, you will not take all the proper steps to lose weight consistently. I understand that there may be some logistics that can be further explained during your journey. However, weight loss is about calories in and calories out. Even if you do not 100% understand the all in all of the calories, we all know veggies are healthy, and most cookies are unhealthy. Yes, I said "MOST" we will later discuss some OK cookies to eat. So, we could simply focus our diet on eating various veggies. Next, we know that our body needs exercise and that the lack of exercise has many adverse effects on our bodies. It is better to find active things to do versus living an inactive lifestyle.

What happens when we stop exercising?

- o   Your muscle fibers start to diminish in size and strength
- o   Your body begins to retain water
- o   Your endurance decreases
- o   Your body starts to break muscle down and increase fat
- o   Your metabolism slows down
- o   More prone to fatigue and lack of sleep
- o   Increased risk for health issues such as high cholesterol, type 2 diabetes, high blood pressure, depression, and insomnia.

For these reasons, I believe exercise is essential. My favorite aspect of exercising, however, is the mental aspect. "Mind over Matter." Since I know, the psychological aspects of working out these are what I like to focus on. I continuously focus on the mental aspect when I deal with myself and attempt to motivate other people. Again, "Mind over Matter." When your esteem, motivation, hope, belief in your weight loss abilities and all these things are in the right place you will Whoop Whoop at times when you don't want to. You will Whoop Whoop at a time when you or someone else said or thought you couldn't. You will Whoop Whoop even when you didn't know you could.

Whoop Whoop
Willpower- I have goals, and no matter what I am going to make sure that I accomplish them.
Hope- I am so happy that I will reach my goals. I can literally see myself living/enjoying life at my goal weight.
Optimistic- I am not going to focus on the things that I can not change. I am going to focus on my positive attributes and use them to help me improve or overcome my shortcomings.
Oath- I promise myself that I am going to live and reach my goals. I must keep my promise to me.
Perseverance- I am lacing up my boots. I am ready for war! Step out my way world! I will reach my goals!

In real life, I am continually speaking about Whoop Whooping. So yes, we will also cover it often in this book. Once the Whoop Whoop mindset is installed. You will be unstoppable. We all know that through repetition, our mind remembers and through repetition, we are able to reprogram our mind… So yes, Whoop Whoop! Whoop Whoop! Whoop Whoop! lol.

In this journey, it's all about FAB… **F**inding your **A**cceptable **B**alance. Meaning finding what works for you. Not letting society, yourself, or anyone else put you in any particular box. If I allowed society to put me in this box, I would not be an obese lady writing a book on how to lose weight. Even though I have lost nearly 200 pounds, society says I am still fat and that I can not tell others how to lose weight. The sad thing is that I almost put myself in this boxed-in mentality too. I remember when I first completed Life Coaching. I told my Instructor Ms. Terri Butler that I wanted to really help others lose weight, but I felt like I needed to reach a goal size before people would listen to me. I needed to be skinny before I was validated to motivate. Bigggggg shouts out to her. It was her words that helped start all of this. She said, "Clarissa because you are big you are relatable. People will listen to you because they know you truly understand how they feel". She too was once on a weight loss journey and had lost 50 pounds herself. So, I accepted this role as being a Fitness Motivator but did not 100% take myself out of the box. When going to events and introducing myself to new people, I felt like I always had to justify why I called myself a Fitness Motivator. I would say, My name is Clarissa Young confidently… then the confidence would dwindle as I said I am a Fitness Motivator, then sometimes the looks would come, then I would start the justification. I would say, "At my heaviest, I was 515 pounds; I was imprisoned in my own body. I've lost x number of pounds blasé blasé blasé". For some, the praise would come, then for some, I was given advice on what I needed to do (as if I didn't know what to do), and some would just look. Either way, it was me allowing society to put me in this box for why I even attempted to explain why I was qualified. If I were 150 pounds with a "Nice" shape, no one would question my ability to motivate. Let's look more in-depth, I am saying I am a Motivator, not an expert, not a guru (lol even though I could be. I definitely know most of the ins and outs… It's just a matter of doing it).

Hey, because I'm 150 pounds does it means I'm a great motivator? What if I've been 150 pounds all my life, always had a healthy relationship with food, been in sports since a kid… Can I really motivate someone who struggles with weight? Maybe, but do I really understand the ins and out of the battles that the average obese person fights mentally, physically, and spiritually daily??? More than likely not. Sometimes, we have to personally go through something to be able to understand where that person is coming from fully. Empathy and sympathy are great from a person, but understanding is the key to really help. There is a saying that goes, "Do not judge a book by its cover." Though to the outside, I might appear unqualified, but until you open up to me and know my story you don't really know my journey. Now, this also goes for that 150 pounds person… because they are this size there very much so could be a story on the inside to tell. Try not to categories people, label, or put in a box. Treat others how you want to be treated. That 150-pound bodybuilder may have been that 400-pound teenager that put sweat and tears to get where he or she is currently at. Loving each other for who they are, getting to know a person before judgment is what our society needs more of. To get society to change it starts with believing in our own self. Stand up and make a change in our own lives, and eventually, society will catch a clue…hopefully. Either way, I have to love me, and you have to love you.

Bible verses to meditate on that will further help with this topic:
- Fear not, for I am with you; be not dismayed, for I am your God; I will strengthen you, I will help you, I will uphold you with my righteous right hand. **Isaiah 41:10**
- Have I not commanded you? Be strong and courageous. Do not be frightened, and do not be dismayed, for the Lord your God is with you wherever you go. **Joshua 1:9**
- When I consider your heavens, the work of your fingers, the moon, and the stars, which you have set in place, what is mankind that you are mindful of them, human beings that you care for them? You have made them a little lower than the angels and crowned them with glory and honor. You made them rulers over the works of your hands; you put everything under their feet: all flocks and herds, and the animals of

the wild, the birds in the sky, and the fish in the sea, all that swim the paths of the seas. **Psalm 8:3-8**

Just do it…

In my opinion, one of the most significant setbacks to weight loss is procrastination. It's rare that someone wakes up today and say I am going to start my journey today. In all actuality, most of us could very well start our journey at that very moment that we decide that we want or need to make a change. If you have breath and plan to eat… You are equipped to start your journey. Many times, we wait for a Monday, for the 1ˢᵗ of the Month, until our friend is ready, after our birthday, and many other crazy reasons. This journey is a lifestyle change. Your change must occur every day of the week. In any month, with or without a friend, and even on your birthday. Often, as we wait to start life occurs. Does this sound familiar?

For some random reason, you get on the scale and notice you have gained 15 pounds since the last time you were on it or maybe you went to put on your favorite dress, and it was too tight and not as flattering as usual. So, you say "Self… I got to get this weight off me. I am tired of being overweight. I am tired of looking like this in the mirror. I just want to be healthy and happy with my body. I am going on a diet" (1ˢᵗ Mistake) I am about to go all in. I'm only doing veggies and fish until I reach the next 50 pounds. (Mistakes 2 and 3) I'm so ready. I never exercise, but because I'm serious I'm going to exercise 6 days a week. (Mistake 4) I am going to start in 2 weeks when I get paid because I can buy my groceries and join the gym. (mistake 5) You are extra excited.

You write out all your goals. You tell everybody that you are going to start for real on Friday when you get paid. You also let yourself splurge a little because things are about to get serious on payday. Time passes, everything is great, and it's the day before payday. Whoop Whoop! About to really get serious tomorrow, Saturday at the latest (because you need time to go to the store after work). Coming home from work on Thursday, your only means of transportation starts to make a clicking sound. Money is tight, so you keep driving without checking it out. Friday morning, we wake up… We weigh ourselves (gained a pound or 2 from splurging… no big deal it's payday). You leave to go to work, and the car simply will not start. I'm sure you know where this is going. Long story short. the money that you would've liked to spend on the gym and extra groceries are now being used to maintain your car. Your frustrated that you are spending unplanned money, you can't start the gym this paycheck, andddddddd you are now heavier than when you first decided to get serious.

Your journey is a lifestyle change, not a quick fix, not a 2-month diet, but a lifestyle change and even if you lose weight when you return back to old habits it will not be long before you put the weight back on. What I'm saying is that you can start your journey with whatever food you have in the house. If all you have is Ramon noodles and green beans, then that's precisely what you eat. Of course, eat the noodles in moderation. Any movement is exercise, it does not have to be at a gym. You can do this! You can do this now!!!

FAB Activity #11/ What's the mistake and then tell why:
Going back into the story, I want you to look at mistakes 1 through 5. List what the mistake is and why it is a mistake in your own words. If you can understand and accept that this is a mistake, it is less likely that you will continue to make the same mistake. If you continue with this behavior, it then goes from a mistake to outright procrastination, and it will be up to you to decide how bad do you really want to reach your goals. Following your explanation, I will give my point of view. We may agree on the point of view, or we may have different opinions. What's most important is that you mentally process how to "JUST DO IT" and actively work at reaching your goals.

In the box below first write out what is the mistake. Then think it out clearly and state why it is a mistake.

Mistake 1:	
Mistake 2:	
Mistake 3:	

Mistake 4:	
Mistake 5:	

For those of you that took the time to really reflect on the mistakes, I am super proud of you. For those that did not reflect. I strongly encourage you to really take the time and do the exercise. You brought the book. You want to change. Give it your all! When we genuinely understand our behaviors and train our thought is when we can begin to correct them. I declare for myself and everyone reading this book that the spirit of procrastination cannot settle within us or within our home. No procrastination may exist, whether it is dealing with health or any other lifestyle areas.

Bible verses to meditate on that will further help with this topic:
- Whoever watches the wind will not plant; whoever looks at the clouds will not reap. **Ecclesiastes 11:4**
- Lazy hands make for poverty, but diligent hands bring wealth. **Proverbs 10:4**
- A sluggard's appetite is never filled, but the desires of the diligent are fully satisfied. **Proverbs 13:4**
- Sluggards do not plow in season; so, at harvest time they look but find nothing. **Proverbs 20:4**

My explanation of Mistakes above.

Mistake 1: Was the thought of going on a "diet".
As stated above this is a journey. This is a lifestyle change. Your journey should include all the foods that you enjoy. The focus on the food should be less on what you consume and

more so on how much you take in. When you look at the food pyramid, it includes all meals. So, let's take a cake, for example. If you like cake, it is very unlikely that you will never eat a slice a cake again. However, it best to practice moderation. Maybe a half slice once a week or however much fits into your calorie budget (later discussed). Also understanding to eat less does not mean to lose weight. You can have a huge bowl of cabbage, and it will not negatively affect you.

Mistake 2: I am only doing veggies and fish.
Not only is this unrealistic for some, but it also does not give you all of the needed nutrition for your body's daily intake. I know personally for myself the moment I say I am going to eat only "X-Y-Z" all hell breaks out. I mean, I may do good for about 3 to 4 days, but then my body goes through all of the withdrawal symptoms from carbs, and it starts a downward spiral. However, the best thing is to include all the food groups, but make healthier options. Carbs are not the enemy. Carbs are what fuel your body. To go without carbs is like driving your car with water versus gas. It needs carbs… Complex carbs. This will consist of your veggies, sweet potatoes, quinoa, brown rice, etc…. Be sure to check out my cheesy quinoa recipe (a great alternative to rice or mac and cheese) in the back of the book.

Symptoms of sugar/carb withdrawal
·   Cravings
·   Obsession
·   Mood swings
·   Fatigue
·   Dizziness
·   Irritability

Mistake 3: I'm not going to stop till I reach 50 pounds
Many will not understand why this is a mistake, because this seems very similar to how many of us set our goals and determine if we are successful or not. Now, it is a great idea to have 50 pounds as your long-term goal, but don't stop there. Break the goal down into measurable goals that you can obtain. Kind of like the example I gave you in chapter 2 regarding the student that wants to earn a bachelor's degree. Once the goal is set. The focus is then set on the steps that are needed to take place daily vs. the end goal. So, let us focus on what we can do daily to reach our goals. Let's also plan to celebrate and reward ourselves along the way.

Mistake 4: I never exercise, but now I'm the 6 days a week.
This is great that we want to get extra serious and jump right in. However, it is more likely that we will exhaust ourselves and give up a lot sooner before we have enough time to make it a habit. It's great to start with smaller goals and work our way up to increase. Also, we want to be sure to address the reason why we never exercise. Are we in pain, do we not have

energy, is it annoying, don't have enough time or we just simply don't want to? Resolve that barrier first, and it will make the goal of committing to a regular workout routine a lot more obtainable.

Mistake 5: I am going to start when….

I think this one was pretty explanatory in the example. Just do it. Just jump right in. Things do not have to be perfect. Tomorrow is not promised. Procrastination is only a delay that often times hinder us from our goals. I know some say if you procrastinate, it's because you don't want it bad enough. Maybe that is true. It also could be that you want it so bad, but you failed so much that deep inside you are terrified. You are afraid that you can't get it done, so we push off and come up with reasons for why we have to wait.

Often times, we are in a rush to hit our goals. While we are rushing, we are doing all the wrong things and actually hindering our progress. For example, not eating to create a calorie deficit or maybe even merely beating ourselves up mentally and or verbally. Once we take the race out of it, we enjoy life and the process itself. With this enjoyment, ironically, we usually by default reach our goals faster than when we push ourselves through misery. A business partner of mine told a story, and it has never left me.

A quick clip of his story that I will never forget…

One day a man decided that he wanted to cut down a tree out of his backyard. So, he decided that every day he would go to the tree and take 5 whacks at it. After so many consistent days of whacking the tree, it fell down. This is because of his consistency. However, many of us with this same scenario would whack someday and some days, not for whatever reason. Maybe it rained that day, or perhaps you didn't feel well. So, you didn't take the couple of minutes it was needed to whack the tree 5 times. Or some of us will whack daily, but after hitting one tree for a couple of days, we STOP. We stop and decide its best to hit a different tree. We were doing well with our diet, but because pounds are still there, we switch and start a new diet. Start a new tree, we now have to rework everything that we have done.

I said all that to turn and say (lol help me say it) … It did not come on overnight and

_____!

Exactly, it's not going to come off overnight. Different people will reach their goals at different paces. Learn to enjoy your journey. If the goal is to make it a lifestyle change, then we often can take some pressure off the end result. WE CAN, AND WE WILL DO THIS!

Calories in Vs. Calories out

At the end of the day, the most important thing to remember while going on your weight loss journey is calories in vs. calories out. With most things in life, we always keep a close eye on what we take in and put out, but when it comes to weight loss it's rare. I once saw this example somewhere, and it made so much sense. Let's think about it this way, you go to work all week. You work hard and long hours. On Friday you get paid. Most of us create a budget. Whether it is a physical budget or a mental one, most of us use some type of guideline on what our money will be spent on. It's basically the same thing with losing weight. We work hard all day to eat the right things, to say no to certain food/drink temptations, then we go beast mode in the gym.

Now to most of us, this sounds great because we are eating right and working out. However, many times we think we are eating right and most of us do not understand the breakdown of macros, how many calories our body needs per day, or how many calories we burned during our workout. This is very important. Yes, we can have great supplements to help us, but in the end, even if you have the best supplements and are eating too much or too little you can impede your progress. Yes, too few calories are not good either. Yes, you may see weight loss on the scale, but what are you really losing. Are you losing fat, water, or muscle? Often times, we do fad diets, and we lose water and muscle. Causing us to slow down our metabolism and also put our bodies into starvation mode.

I'll never forget this set of hamsters I had when I was thirteen years old. They taught me so much. Unfortunately for them, I was not the best at taking care of them. I was to them as some of us are to our bodies. I would go days without feeding them. Then, when I finally remembered I would overfeed them. Many of us do the same thing with our bodies. We go all day without eating, then the body lets us know we are hungray... not a typo I meant hungray because we are past hungry. Then we eat and often times overeat. Now my hamsters did precisely what your body does after I finally fed them. These hamsters would take the food that should have lasted them for the next 2-3 days and rid all of it in one serving. Notice I said rid... not eat. They would eat some of it, but most of it they would stuff in their cheeks and keep it there for later. Our bodies do the same thing. After we go for hours, some of us for days without eating our bodies go into starvation mode. We use the food to supply a few needs, but most of it is stored away for a rainy day. Our body stores the food because it does not know the next time, we will feed it. Unfortunately, it is not stored away as lean muscle, but it is stored as fat. Fat is what fuels our bodies. When ingesting fatty food, fat is not the enemy as long as you are eating it in the right form and the right quantities. This will explain why sometimes some people eat only once a day, but still can't seem to lose weight.

With that being said, I am not against intermittent fasting. I love intermittent fasting. In my mind, intermittent fasting is basically an eating schedule of periods of when you do and do not eat. I like to set my fasting period from 9 pm to 1 pm. You do not eat until after your fasting window is over. I allow myself to eat 3 to 4 times within an 8-hour window from 1 pm to 9 pm. Now, these are not 3 to 4 large meals. This consist of 2 to 3 meals with 1 to 2 snacks. With a focus on veggies and protein. With a few added complex carbs. With that being said, I too have my times when I veer off from my goals. However, my goals are still set each day and I get a little stronger and stronger. Each day I get a bit more discipline. It is better to have a goal and notice that you have fallen off course versus to have no goal and to continually be off course. I remember when I first started fasting, I could barely make it to 10 am before I was eating. Now sometimes I look up, and it is 12:30 pm, and I am preparing for my 1ˢᵗ meal of the day. With time, things get more comfortable. Many ask why I like fasting from 1 pm to 9 pm vs. 10 am to 6 pm or 8 am to 4 pm. I love the later fast because I am an evening eater. This way, I am intentionally setting my schedule for later, rather than eating early. Spending all my calories during the day to still eat more in the evening.

FAB Activity #12/ Calories in vs calories out:

So, let's talk about that statement. Spending Calories. In this next assignment, you will learn just how many calories you have to spend daily. You will learn to set a calorie budget. No worries once you understand the logistics of it, please know that there are hundreds of free apps that will do the math for you; much easier and quicker.

How to calculate the calorie budget:

First, figure your Basal Metabolic Rate (BMR) this is the number of energy /calories your body needs at rest. If you did absolutely nothing all day but slept in the bed, then your BMR is how many calories your body needs to adequately fuel your everyday needs such as breathing, heart pumping, brain functioning, etc.

The most successful formula is the Harris-Benedict formula. (__Again, you can find an app for this__)

Adult male: 66 + (6.3x bodyweight in lbs.) + (12.9 x height in inches) – (6.8 x age in years) =BMR

Adult female: 655 + (4.3 x weight in lbs.) + (4.7 x height in inches) – (4.7 x age in years) = BMR

Example: A 37-year-old woman weighs 250pounds, and is 5 feet 5 inches

655+ (4.3 x 250) + (4.7 x 65 inches) – (4.7 x 37 years) = BMR

655+ (1075) + (305.5)- (173.9) = BMR

1, 861.6 = BMR

Meaning if this young lady did absolutely nothing all day her body would still burn 1,861.6 calories a day.

Now once you have your BMR because none of us (reading this book) are doing absolutely nothing a day, we must incorporate the calories in which we will burn doing activities to get an actual total daily calorie need.

1. If you do little to no exercise daily: Daily Calorie Need =BMR x 1.2

2. If you do light activity (meaning 1-3 times a week): Daily Calorie Need =BMR x 1.375

3. If you do a moderate activity (meaning 3-5 times a week): Daily Calorie Need =BMR x 1.55

4. If you do a hard activity (meaning 6-7 times a week): Daily Calorie Need =BMR x 1.725

Example: the 37-year-old woman above exercises for 45 -60 minutes 4 times a week.

BMR X 1.55

1, 861.6 x 1.55= 2,885.45 Caloric need per day

So, the young lady above needs to eat/drink 2,885.45 per day to maintain her weight. Since many of our goals is to lose weight, she must then decide how many pounds she wants to lose a week. If she wants to lose the recommended 2 pounds per week, she needs to decrease her intake by 7,000 a week. (Every pound equals 3,500 calories. So, to get 2 pounds multiply 3500x2)

Now take 7, 000 calories a week and divide it by 7 days. The lady above needs to eat 1000 fewer calories a day to lose 2 pounds by the end of the week. Making her daily calorie goal 1,1885.

YOUR TURN:

Calculate your daily Calorie need to lose 2 pounds per week. 2 pounds lost per week equals 104 pounds lost in one year!!! You can use the formula above or an app. With all this being said, 100% of your focus should not be on the scale. This is a guide to put you on the right path. You want to focus on your food consumption, exercise, water intake, sleep, medication, and such daily to hit your goals. The scale will fluctuate very often. The scale does not know the difference between when you gain muscle, lose water, or lose fat… Always calculate your inches as well.

Put your Daily Calorie Needs here_____

Below you will see a great illustration on where to take your body measurements and which measurements are good to keep track of during weight loss.

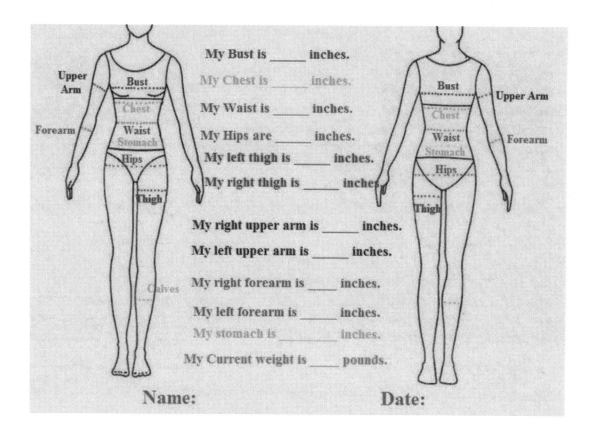

My Bust is _____ inches.

My Chest is _____ inches.

My Waist is _____ inches.

My Hips are _____ inches.

My left thigh is _____ inches.

My right thigh is _____ inches.

My right upper arm is _____ inches.

My left upper arm is _____ inches.

My right forearm is _____ inches.

My left forearm is _____ inches.

My stomach is _____ inches.

My Current weight is _____ pounds.

Name: Date:

Bible verses to meditate on that will further help with this topic:

- For I know the plans I have for you, declares the Lord, "plans to prosper you and not to harm you, plans to give you hope and a future." **Jeremiah 29:11**

- What, then, shall we say in response to these things? If God is for us, who can be against us? **Romans 8:31**

- Be on your guard; stand firm in faith; be courageous; be strong. **1 Corinthians 16:13**

I know someone is like, I thought she said we can have cookies... LOL. Yes, I did say not all cookies are fatty cookies. Along my journey, I am meeting some extraordinary people. One of them is Mrs. Sally, and she is one of my FAB Sisters. I call her my Keto Queen. Mrs. Sally taught me that I can have my cake and eat it too. In the past, I never felt the need to completely deprived myself. Before, my thinking was instead of having a full slice of cake have a few bites. In addition to that, I now know ingredients are key. Let's say if you are a rice lover. Ok, no problem. Have brown rice instead of white rice. So back to the cookies. With the swapping of some ingredients flour, sugar, etc. you can turn your average cookie into a healthier alternative. With that being said, too much of anything can be bad for you. Take a look in Chapter 9 for a few of my favorite recipes. Yes, you will find keto cookies back there.

FAB

Chapter 4 When to Start

The only thing left to do is JUST DO IT. At this point, I'm not sure if starting is the easiest or if it is the hardest part of your fitness journey. However, I do know that it is the most important part. You can understand and plan everything but never start. You can be at your breaking point, feeling down and out, but never begin. If you never start, it is a fact that you will never get it done. So, your best option is to just jump right in and start. You can start whether you know what you are doing or if you have no clue what to do. I can promise you that you will get closer to your goal, having no clue on what you are doing versus knowing everything but never starting.

For many of us, our weight loss journey is more than just a number on the scale or more than only fitting into a sexy dress. Our weight affects our self-esteem, hope, belief values, support system, and more. I can hear someone saying if they don't want to support me while I'm big, then don't support me at all. I totally agree with you.... But how many people have you isolated yourself from due to not being at your fitness goal? How many events have you stayed home from due to low self-esteem that you may have met your next support partner? Or any other guilt that comes with not being at your goal weight? Notice I'm saying "not at goal weight" versus being overweight. This is because whether you need to lose 5 pounds, or you need to lose 300 pounds; everyone is affected differently at different levels along their personal journey.

Let's look at a young lady that has been slim all her life. Let's put a number to it! She has been, on average of 135 pounds most of her life. Now life starts to happen, the last couple of years of her life have been rough, or maybe even she was living her best life; possibly she had a baby. Either way, she gets on the scale to find out that she put on 15 pounds. So, with her new added pounds, she now weighs a whopping 150 pounds. Now, for Clarissa who once weighed 515 pounds, that 150 on the scale sounds A-mazing. For this young lady, the extra 15 pounds hurt her joints and back. She barely can fit some of her favorite clothes. People have started to point out the fact that she put on weight. To make matters worse, her High

School 10 year class reunion is 1 week away. Does she go and hope others don't notice she put on the extra weight, or does she stay home because she is too embarrassed? How many things in your life have you missed out on because you have not hit your fitness goal? (***write them down***)

· High School Reunions

· Birthday Parties

· Family Reunions

· Theme Parks

· Family Trips

The bad news is you can never get those days back. The great news is today is a new day. I'm going to say that again, and I need you to say it and thank God for it. Today is a new day! That means you can now create memories and accomplish any dream that your heart desires. As long as you have air in your lungs; anything is possible. Take this advice from a woman who was once 515 pounds. I was imprisoned in my own body. I was ashamed to look in full-size mirrors. I would hurt when I walked for over five minutes. If I went to places, I needed to know if they had chairs. If they had chairs, then I needed to know did the chairs had arms. If they had no arms, before this outing could be approved I still needed to know how sturdy were the chairs and how far did I have to walk to get to the chair.

I remember the anxiety that came with going to a party, and it being limited chairs there. Many times, events had more people than they had chairs. It's like you are scared to go to the bathroom or anywhere else because you don't want your chair to be taken when you get back. So, not only was I limited to the events I could attend, but I also found myself chair bound at most events. Don't even talk about those little white fold up chairs; that's another story. I would put those chairs up against the wall and pray that I would be able to catch myself if it decided to give in.

Talk about the mental anxiety of just trying to chill at a party. Being at a party and can barely laugh or move because you are afraid that your life support, AKA the chair is going to give out on you. Guys I've been there, and I am not there today. I thank God, and I know he is the only reason why my life has changed. I can now go to parties and can stand. I can walk to events. In fact, I may complain, but I have walked in about five 5K races. Yes

Yes! Your life can change! God is just waiting for you to allow him to come in and help you with this matter.

"The graveyard is the richest place on earth, because it is here that you will find all the hopes and dreams that were never fulfilled, the books that were never written, the songs that were never sung, the inventions that were never shared, the cures that were never discovered, all because someone was too afraid to take that first step, keep with the problem, or determined to carry out their dream."

- Les Brown

"The whole idea of motivation is a trap. Forget motivation. Just do it. Exercise, lose weight, test your blood sugar, or whatever. Do it without motivation. And then, guess what? After you start doing the thing, that's when the motivation comes and makes it easy for you to keep on doing it." ~ John C. Maxwell

"You may delay, but time will not." ~ Benjamin Franklin

What are you waiting for?

When speaking to people, I often ask… Why not start today? The typical answers I get are: I don't want to fail, I don't know what to do, waiting on a particular time to pass, I don't have time, etc., etc., etc…. We have addressed "I don't know what to do" and "waiting on a special time" in Chapter 3. Now we will look more into "I don't want to fail" and "I don't have time."

I don't want to fail:

I have spoken with people before, and they said, Clarissa, I have dieted so much, and I did not lose weight I also do not want to try anymore. They say I don't want to try anymore because I know that I will not succeed. My response to them and anyone reading this that feels the same way is… Ok! … So, if you tried to lose weight, you might lose, or you might win. Meaning you may try and not lose weight, or you may try and actually lose a few pounds! However, if you do not try to lose weight, you will continue to be where you are or possibly get further out of shape. So, if you are truly unhappy with how you feel why not try. Be a risk-taker. Live life! Now I am not saying to risk everything or to risk crazy stuff. I am saying to take the risk in believing in yourself and even more so take the risk to believe in God. Look at your odds. The odds are in your favor. If you win. You win, but if you lose, you have not lost anything. You simply stay where you are, and you live another day to fight again (Lol, in my pops voice from the movie Friday).

Let's be serious... I really think that the most significant issue comes from the lose or win notion. Let's look at what does it truly mean to lose. You decide that you want to diet, you try to diet, you eat things you are not supposed to eat, and you do not lose weight. Did you really lose? No, as long as you try, you are on the winning bench. It's like that tree in the woods that we are trying to knockdown. The first couple of whacks may not do anything to the tree. It may even take 100 blows before you start to put a good indent in the tree. However, if you keep trying, one day you will knock the tree down. This journey is about making lifestyle changes. It should not be looked at as a race to get slim.

Let's not rush life or rush the process. Some of us get so tied up in the race that we forget to enjoy the scenery. We are so stuck on the finish line that sometimes when we get there, we don't even take the time to really celebrate because it's on to the next race. You said you wanted to lose 10 pounds by your birthday. You broke your neck to lose them ten pounds!!! Your birthday is barely over, and all you can think about is the next 50 pounds that you have to lose. No celebration of what you completed. No appreciation for what was done by the grace of God in which you have accomplished. It's straight on to the next race. Along your journey, you do not win or lose. In this journey, you LIVE, or you live. You LIVE your best life, or you will merely exist.

Whether you try to live your best life or not, time will continue to pass you by. Your birthday will continue to come. Life around you will continue to take place. This is when we have to put our big girl/big boy undies on and decide whether I am going to live my life or am I going to let life live me. I have had people ask me all the time how I gain my confidence to get started. And unfortunately, no one can help you with this area, but you and the man up above (God). Confidence increases with success. Success comes with trial and error. The error comes with at least first trying. Trying comes with having faith that you will be able to finish. Check your faith. Are you looking for "you" to help you? Or are you looking for the man who knows all, sees all and can do all (God) to help you? To try and in return not achieve your goal is not considered a failure in my book. I am sure that there is something that you will gain from the experience that you can turn into a positive to help you do better next time. How many of us dated an Ex? You tried all you could to make it work. He or she just would not do right by you. That relationship had to end prematurely. Years later, you meet the love of your life. Now you are better prepared for the real deal because in that "no deal" relationship you learned or developed something. Lol, I thank one of my ex's. I won't put any names, but because of him I now know how to sweep. LMBO. Yes, he showed me the proper way to hold a broom and sweep the floor. Before him, I was just doing it all wrong and working myself extra hard trying to sweep up the dirt.

I know some of y'all are like girl... What did you not know about sweeping? He taught me that you don't put the broom directly on top of the trash you are sweeping, instead, you extend it a few inches ahead to gather. Lol. I just taught somebody too... So now my husband has a wife that can sweep. Lol, but for real. You only fail when you do not try. To get your confidence to "start this thing" is to simply JUST START. Jump in! Do not look back… Just start. I wish I could literally push or shake some people to just start. Then, if things don't go right give them a hug and a slap on the butt to jump right back in the journey. This thing called life. We got this, but not until we truly believe that we can do this!

If you look at this thing as a race, just know that the race you are running is not your fitness journey. Your race is the time you have here on earth. This race of life can be looked at as a relay race. You know the race where you run as fast as you can, then you pass the baton to someone else. That person will pick up the next part of the race, then pass it to the next person in line. The only difference is you are the only one running, and you are passing the baton back to yourself. So either you walk, run, or crawl. Only you can do it and "You" are waiting for you to get to the next hurdle.

FAB Activity #13/ To try or not to try; Pros vs. Cons:

If you find that you are the one that just cannot get started because you don't think you can be successful, then no problem this next activity is for you. I want you to create a list. On the left side, I want you to write if you try and you succeed what will you gain. Maybe you will gain confidence, energy, faith, or endurance. If you try and you do not reach your goal (this go around) what could you possibly lose? Write this on the right side of the paper. Maybe you may lose the money you spend at the grocery store or you lose the time it took you to meal prep. I want you to really spend time on this activity.

If I try what could I possibly gain?	If I try what could I possibly lose?

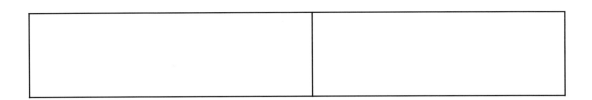

Now that your list is done, I want you to look at your list. Is it worth trying? Do you win or lose more when you try? 9 out of 10 people will win more when they try. The other 10 percent may need to rethink their goals. If reaching after your goals do not create a win for you, then why is it even a goal?

Bible verses to meditate on that will further help with this topic:

- Whatever the activity in which you engage, do it with all your ability because there is no work, no planning, no learning, and no wisdom in the next world where you're going. **Ecclesiastes 9:10**

- Let's not get tired of doing what is good, for, at the right time, we will reap a harvest—if we do not give up. **Galatians 6:9**

- I have fought the good fight. I have completed the race. I have kept the faith. **2 Timothy 4:7**

- Surely you know that many runners take part in a race, but only one of them wins the prize. Run, then, in such a way as to win the prize. Every athlete in training submits to strict discipline, in order to be crowned with a wreath that will not last; but we do it for one that will last forever. That is why I run straight for the finish line; that is why I am like a boxer who does not waste his punches. I harden my body with blows and bring it under complete control, to keep myself from being disqualified after having called others to the contest. **1 Corinthians 9:24-27**

- Commit your work to the Lord, then it will succeed. Proverbs 16:3

I don't have time

One of the most common obstacles that many people ask for my advice is finding the time. Especially, when it comes to exercising, they do not have the time to exercise or to cook healthy meals. My honest feedback to that is, you have to make time for you. Overall, it really is an excuse or procrastination. 9 out of 10 people do have the time. It is simply that their fitness journey is not a priority. It can also fall into that all or nothing type of attitude. If I don't have time to meal prep, that means that I must eat unhealthily. There are always healthy eating options available on the go.

The healthiest food we can eat comes from the earth and packs the most nutrition is raw veggies. Even if you have no time to cook, it takes a few seconds to grab fruits or veggies and pack them in your lunch. Also, these days many restaurants, even fast-food restaurants have accepted a healthy trend. Most restaurants sell salad or grilled food. The next rebuttal to that is that it is expensive to eat healthily. Eggs, wheat bread, fresh veggies, and chicken are obtainable for most budgets. So, the question really falls back on, how bad do you want to be fit? What is your "why"?

So back to not having time to work out. Again, it does not have to be an all or nothing type of attitude. To work out does not mean that you have to go to the gym and spend hours upon hours. A walk for lunch, squats in the restroom, using stairs instead of the elevator, and parking in the furthest parking spot are all ways to fit some type of exercise into your daily routine. If you were first starting your journey and was not exercising at all, your body will appreciate even the smallest amount of movement. After we start adding movements, our habits will begin to form, making it easier to add even more movements at a later time.

FAB Activity #14/ What are you doing?

In this next activity, you will write down your current schedule. I want you to focus on the average daily schedule that you have, not the schedule that you wish to have. If it changes week to week, that's ok. Use what you do know. Perhaps your schedule changes but you requested every Friday off; write that. Be sure to include everything from when you wake up to when you go to bed.

Here is an example of what your schedule should look like. Notice every waking hour of the day is consumed by doing something.

Time	Sunday	Monday	Tuesday	Wednesday	Thursday	Friday	Saturday

7:00 am	Sleep	Shower	Shower	Shower	Shower	Shower	Sleep
8:00 am	Shower	Mediate and read Bible	Mediate and read Bible	Mediate and read Bible	Mediate and read Bible	Mediate and read Bible	Sleep
9:00 am	Breakfast / Travel to Church	Breakfast / Travel to work	Breakfast / Travel to work	Breakfast / Travel to work	Breakfast / Travel to work	Breakfast / Travel to work	Shower
10:00 am	Church	Work	Work	Work	Work	Work	Breakfast
11:00 am							Clean Home
12:00 pm							Kim Babyshower
1:00 pm	Out to eat with family						
2:00 pm							
3:00 pm	Meal Prep for the week						Do Kids hair and get uniforms laid out for school
4:00 pm	Do Laundry						
5:00 pm	Set Schedule for next week						

6:00 pm	Check emails						Cook dinner and eat as a Family at the table
7:00 pm	Special Time with Hubby	Homework/ Family time	Homework/ Family time	Homework/ Family time	Homework/ Family time	Movie Night	
8:00 pm	Prepare for bed	Prepare for bed	Prepare for bed	Prepare for bed	Prepare for bed		Date night with hubby

Next, write down your "why". Why are you on your fitness journey. What is it do you want to gain or prevent from happening?

<table>
<tr><td></td></tr>
<tr><td></td></tr>
<tr><td></td></tr>
</table>

Now that you have your "why". It is time to make time for you. It is time to make this journey of yours a priority. We only get one body. One-shot at life. How we treat this body does make a difference. If you find that after completing your schedule there is absolutely no time for you to work on you, it's time to pray. Pray that God removes some distractions from your life and that he gives you the time to take care of his temple. Keep in mind that sometimes to fit things in your schedule you may have to move some things around, and you may also have to do things against the grain. Here is an example: many people do laundry on the weekend. Maybe doing laundry Wednesday at lunchtime fits better into your schedule than the weekend. You may have to add some activities together or delegate some tasks to other members involved in your life. Maybe you make your 10-year-old daughter lunch every day. How about allowing her to make her lunch, but randomly you can create a quick "I love you note" and place it with her lunch. Now she gained some independence, and she is reminded that mommy or daddy loves her too.

Create your schedule. This schedule will work for all. Whether you work overnight, during the day, or do not clock in at all. (Extra schedules are in the back of the book)

Time	Sunday	Monday	Tuesday	Wednesday	Thursday	Friday	Saturday
12:00 am							
1:00 am							
2:00 am							
3:00 am							
4:00 am							
5:00 am							
6:00 am							
7:00 am							
8:00 am							
9:00 am							

10:00 am						
11:00 am						
12:00 pm						
1:00 pm						
2:00 pm						
3:00 pm						
4:00 pm						
5:00 pm						
6:00 pm						
7:00 pm						
8:00 pm						

9:00 pm							
10:00 pm							
11:00 pm							

Bible verses to meditate on that will further help with this topic:

- Teach us to number our days, that we may gain a heart of wisdom. **Psalm 90:12**

- So we do not focus on what is seen, but on what is unseen. For what is seen is temporary, but what is unseen is eternal. **2 Corinthians 4:18**

- For which of you, wanting to build a tower, doesn't first sit down and calculate the cost to see if he has enough to complete it? **Luke 14:28**

- A person plans his way, but the LORD directs his steps. **Proverbs 16:9**

12 Time Management Hacks

1. Create a plan

Plan your time ahead. Use a calendar to thoroughly plan out your day, week, month, and even your year. Be sure to revisit your plan often. Mark Everything on your calendar. Giving it a start and end time. These days they even have it where you can sync your calendar on your phone. This also gives you the option to link all members of the family calendars together. This way, everyone knows what everyone is doing. This should help avoid double-booking mommy or daddy for activities.

2. Know your deadlines

When do you need to finish your tasks? Mark the periods out clearly in your calendar/ organizer. This will help you stay on track when you need to complete them. Prioritize your to-do list using the Urgent Vs. Important Matrix. What box does your activity fall in? Put it on your schedule if important or urgent. Keep it off your schedule if neither important or urgent.

	Urgent	_Not Urgent_
Important	Do First ❖ Tasks that require immediate attention	Do later ❖ Tasks that need action but not immediate attention.
Not Important	Delegate ❖ Tasks that require immediate action but do not contribute to your goals.	Eliminate ❖ Tasks that are neither important nor urgent.

3. Eliminate. A.K.A- Learn to say "No."

Don't take on more than you can handle. When distractions come about, and it does not benefit you or the ones that you are responsible for, then the best thing to do is pass and say no. You can always defer it to a later period. This goes for saying no to yourself as well as to others.

4. Delegate

If there are things that can be done by others or things that are not so important, consider delegating. This takes a load off your back, and you can focus on the essential tasks that must be done by you. When you delegate some of your work, you free up your time and in the end, you can achieve more.

5. Have a clock visibly placed before you

Sometimes we are so engrossed in the work that we lose track of time. Having a grasp of the time will better help you to keep track of your timing. Stick to the time that you allotted for each task.

6. Target to be early

When you target to be on time, you'll either be on time or late. Most of the time, you'll be late. However, if you aim to be early, you'll most likely be on time.

For appointments, strive to be early. For your deadlines, submit them earlier than required. Get familiar with setting reminders. Use alarms to remind you of the day before an event. Also, setting a reminder 15- 30 minutes before a task is always productive. Generally, if it is a task that I have to dress up for or drive too, I set my reminder with enough time for me to get dressed, drive, and arrive early. I set my reminder with the intent of preparing me for an event that I may have 100% forgot that I planned to do. So, if I totally forgot about it and it's a dinner date, 15 Minutes before is not enough time to get ready. My reminder should give me time to pick out clothes, get dressed, and drive to the location.

7. Focus

In these times, we take pride in multi-tasking. Unfortunately, our brain responds better when we focus on one activity at a time. We do a bunch of things at one time, never really giving anything our 100% best. Think you are a great multi-tasker. Can you talk about one conversation and type about another at the same time? Are you great at the pat your head, rub your belly, and have a full unrelated conversation at the same time? Lol. I know some of you, I will never be able to convivence that multi-tasking is not the way. That's totally ok, my job is just to inform you. Now for those that believe in not putting all your eggs in one basket. I AGREE. What I am saying is use time blocking. Meaning, set aside an amount of time for each task that you need to complete. After that task time is up, you put it aside and focus on the next. Example, while I am writing this book, that is all that I am doing. I am not writing the book, cooking dinner, and creating a workout plan all at the same time. Though all these things get done in one day, they are on different time blocks. Be sure to block out all distractions such as messages, social media, phone calls, etc.; should be ignored. Lol. I promise most situations can wait until after you finish your current task to be addressed.

8. Don't fuss about unimportant details

To work in excellence and to be a perfectionist, in my opinion, are two different things. Giving it your all the very first time should limit how many times you have to redo something. When repeating an activity, weigh out your benefits of the time invested in redoing vs. the benefits of having the task redone. Lol, have you ever had someone do your hair and they keep doing the part over? They fixed the part 5 times before they start to braid or style. Sus it looks fine to me… Please finish my head… lol

9. Join similar tasks together

Let's say you're going to Walmart. Great, go grocery shopping and whatever other shopping at that store at the same time. Need to clean? Do laundry and clean the kitchen together. While doing these activities, your mind is working in the same pattern. A poor example of joining unlike tasks would be creating your grocery list and exercising at the same time. To create your list, you need to sit and focus. To exercise is to be pumped and engaged. Lol crazy example, but you get my drift.

10. Eliminate your time wasters

What takes your time away from your work? Is it Facebook, Twitter, text, or email that takes up a big part of your day? If so, try checking them less frequently.

I know I myself spend plenty of time on these platforms. The good thing is I also get paid from using them. So, for those that are not getting paid to use them and it is merely for leisure activity, then one thing you can do is make it harder to check them so often – remove them from sight. Many of these things we have shortcuts to on our phones and other devices making it easy to check them, without even having to put much effort into it. It's like you go to check the time, and look you have 20 Facebook notifications. You can turn off notifications and get rid of shortcuts. Out of sight, out of mind. This way you still have access to your accounts, but hopefully, you will find that you check them less frequently.

11. Leave buffer time in-between

Don't schedule tasks back to back. Leave a 5-10-minute buffer time in between each task. This helps you wrap up the previous task and start the next one on time.

12. Stick to the plan

Now that you have a schedule, everybody and they momma are going to call, invite, and/or need you. Limit how often you veer away from your schedule. Else wise, you just wasted all the time that you took to create your schedule. Stick to the plan!

Chapter 5 Getting Support

Doing your fitness journey alone is very doable, but it is not necessary. Many people often say I wish I had a supportive partner, or I wish "I had a workout buddy". My answer to that is you do!!! Today in life if you want to build relationships, there are always people around you that are also wanting the same thing. The problem today is that many people believe in "no new friends" or people have the right expectations from the wrong people. Also, often when people are expecting support, they see it from a one-way street perspective. Many times, they look to people that can help them for support, but in return do not look at how they can be of help to that person.

I am here to help so, read on. Read the next scenario and let's see if this sound familiar for yourself or maybe someone you know. Two friends that have a good relationship and have been friends for a while. One friend is a single mom with older children. The other friend is married with little children. Let's give them names Sally (single) and Mary (married). Sally has been on her fitness journey for about two years. She has a great exercise routine. Mary just had a baby and has struggled the last couple of years to find a balance between having babies, being a wife, a mother, and working on her fitness goals. Mary admires Sally's fitness stability, so she asks her for help. She goes to Sally and tells Sally, I want to work out with you. Sally says, great. Mary tells Sally I really need your help. I need you to make sure I come to the workout with you. Sally agrees. They talk briefly and a schedule is created for them to work out together.

Now, I'm sure for many of us this sounds like a friend helping a friend and that's what it is. A friend helping a friend. The issue is recognizing that it is a 2 part friendship. In many cases, your friend will be more than willing to help you. However, I'm sure that there is something that your friend may also need help with. Be sure to at least offer your help in return of the favor. List off a few of your strong points and see if your friend can use your help.

Mary thanks Sally for her help in advance. Mary agrees to workout at a time that is convenient for Sally. Mary replies, hey Sis I appreciate your support and I want to help you too! Based on the conversation, it is brought to Mary's attention that Sally's daughter needs help with her Algebra homework. It just so happens that Mary is great at math and in return will help Sally's daughter with her algebra. Another way to help maybe on the days of workout Mary can pick her daughter up from school and meet at the house since they are going to work out together anyway. Those are just some examples. It takes a village to raise a child and it takes a village to lose weight. Let's all support and help others in the areas that we can provide help.

Support in the right places

Going back to that last sentence in the prior passage. It says, "lets all support and help others in the areas that we **CAN** provide help". Many times, people are willing to help, but we ask for the right help from the wrong person. Oftentimes, when we ask for help, we ask for help from those who we feel comfortable with. Sally and Marry are both on their Fitness journey. Sally and Marry both struggle with eating clean. So, they decide to tackle this beast together. From one perspective, it looks like a perfect plan. We both struggle with eating right, so let's help each other. However, if I struggle too it's more likely that I can not give you the reinforcement that you need. I can't give you the best reinforcement because I struggle too with eating healthy.

Unfortunately, though we are good friends because I am weak in this area, I will not be the best accountability partner. Not saying that the two cannot help each other, just saying the person you seek to hold you accountable for a goal should be someone that can do just that. They can hold you accountable. Nine times out of ten if I have a weakness for candy bars it is less likely that when I see you eating a candy bar that I will give you an evil eye or remind you of your "why." It is more likely that you will offer me a bite of the candy bar and that we will both eat it. Your accountability partner should be someone that you respect and someone who does great at what you're trying to improve on.

After you pick your accountability person, next it's imperative that you discuss what support looks like. Many people view support in different ways. Because the support is misinterpreted, it can often seem like it is not there. Let's take a husband and wife. The wife is on her fitness journey, and the husband has agreed to help. Nothing else is further discussed. 3 to 4 days go by, and nothing else has been mentioned about the support system. On the 4th day, the wife is eating a Snickers bar, so the husband nicely tells her, she should not eat the Snickers bar. He is supporting her by trying to help her make better decisions. However, her guilt kicks in and she becomes offensive. Its only one snickers bar. I can have one bar. He gives her a look of shame and walks away. In the husband mind he is thinking "she asked for my help and now I am trying to help her". In the wife's mind, she is saying "he has been sitting back waiting on me to do something wrong. I asked him 4 days ago to help me with my journey, and he has not been supportive, but as soon as I eat the wrong thing here he comes...".

Now, let's take a pause and look more into this situation. The husband truly thinks he is helping, the wife really wants the help, but feels as if she is being put down versus being supported. Speaking to that wife, one might ask "what does support look like to you?" She may say, working out with her, giving her praise throughout the day, sending a special text to remind her that she is loved, and maybe even helping her meal prep. Then, one may take the husband to the side and ask him "if you wanted someone to help you on your fitness journey what would you like for them to do?" The husband's reply is to stop me from doing wrong and help me catch my mistakes. So here you have 2 different people, both are wanting support, but having different perspectives on what support is. It is always best to discuss your expectations with your support system.

Tips on receiving the right support:

1. Finding the right person- Find someone who is experienced in the area in which you want to receive support. Someone who knows a little more than you, who is a little stronger than you in this area, or who has experienced more than you have in this area.
2. Know what you want- When you can ask for help, It's only fair to the other person that you yourself know what you want help with. Can you verbalize exactly what you want help with?
3. Have a dialog with the person in which you want to receive help.- Really talk about what, and why you need support. Talk to them about what helps and hurts you. Let them talk about how they can comfortably help you. Throughout the process continue to have communication. You may even have to revamp your support agreement.
4. Try to find something in which you can help them, if applicable.

FAB Activity #15/ Go get help

In this next activity, you will use the steps above to arrange your accountability agreement. Remember your list of accountability partners that you listed in chapter 2? After reviewing this information, you may find that you have to rethink your accountability partner. Once you are content with your 3 accountability partners, it is time to talk with them and see if they agree to help. Now, when seeking accountability partners, how you ask makes a big difference in how much people will commit to you. If you simply say, I need you to make sure I exercise… you may not get that far. How about saying something more like Heyyy Shelia. I love the way you dance. You are so great at it, and you look like you were really having fun. Girl, I need some of that fun in my life. I need to exercise, and I would love it if we can do this together. (Don't inconvenience them) What days do you dance? I would like to join you (Not can you dance with me on Tuesday night. Tuesday nights maybe the night she prefers to rest). Because she wants to help you, she may agree a time or two, but after it becomes an inconvenience, she may be less likely to be available. This also makes it less likely that she will try to persuade or reach out to you when you don't feel like coming. She may say, "oh she doesn't feel like exercising today? Excellent because I'm tired too, I worked a double on Monday and missed my Tuesdays relax days".

You will need to find a way to work your schedule into their schedule. THIS IS YOUR JOURNEY, and you are asking for their help. Use the above steps to speak with your accountability partner.

After you have talked with them and followed all the above steps, put your accountability partners name, best availability time, and in which way they will help you. If applicable, put in what way you will help them. Set goals with your accountability partner. How often will you speak, what will be discussed? Reward yourself and your accountability partner for following through with the plan.

Partner #1
Who is your accountability Partner?

_____

What time and day of the week are they available to follow up or help you?

_____

_____

_____

_____

What are your goals? In what way will your accountability partner help you?

_____

_____

_____

_____

_____

_____

_____

_____

_____

_____

_____

_____

What have you told your accountability partner that you will not perceive as help? Or what things have the accountability partner said that they cannot or will not help you with?

_____

_____

_____

_____

_____

_____

_____

How will you help your accountability partner (if applicable; Remember you can only help in an area that you are stronger than them)

_____

_____

_____

_____

_____

_____

_____

_____

_____

What does your goal look like when it has been achieved? How will you both celebrate?

_____

_____

_____

_____

_____

_____

_____

_____

_____

_____

_____

Partner #2
Who is your accountability Partner?

_____

What time and day of the week are they available to follow up or help you?

_____

_____

_____

_____

_____

What are your goals? In what way will your accountability partner help you?

_____

_____

_____

_____

_____

_____

_____

_____

_____

What have you told your accountability partner that you will not perceive as help? Or what things have the accountability partner said that they cannot or will not help you with?

_____

_____

_____

_____

_____

_____

_____

How will you help your accountability partner (if applicable; Remember you can only help in an area that you are stronger than them)

_____

_____

_____

_____

_____

_____

What does your goal look like when it has been achieved? How will you both celebrate?

_____

_____

_____

_____

_____

_____

_____

_____

_____

_____

_____

_____

Partner #3
Who is your accountability Partner?

_____

What time and day of the week are they available to follow up or help you?

_____

_____

_____

_____

What are your goals? In what way will your accountability partner help you?

_____

_____

_____

_____

_____

_____

_____

_____

_____

What have you told your accountability partner that you will not perceive as help? Or what things have the accountability partner said that they cannot or will not help you with?

_____

_____

_____

_____

_____

_____

_____

How will you help your accountability partner (if applicable; Remember you can only help in an area that you are stronger than them)

_____

_____

_____

_____

_____

_____

_____

What does your goal look like when it has been achieved? How will you both celebrate?

_____

_____

_____

_____

_____

_____

_____

_____

_____

_____

_____

_____

_____

_____

_____

Support Vs. Crutch

Many times in life, we come across people that have our best interests in hearts and they want to help us so much. In fact, they want to help us so much that they want to do everything for us to make sure we get it right. What can happen is, instead of them being someone that supports us along our journey, they become the person that does it for us and can become a crutch. For example, many people are having gastric sleeve surgery, and for some of us it is a great help, and for others, later you will see it really was a crutch. Now let me express that I did have the gastric sleeve surgery in 2014. (The gastric sleeve is when your stomach organ is cut and you no longer can use about 3/4th of it. This drastically cuts how much you can eat in one serving; causing you to lose weight). I have no regrets, and it was the best thing to happen to me. However, as many say before you have the operation, it is a tool to help you through the journey. Many people use the sleeve as THE TOOL and not a tool. Hence, many people sometimes regain after weight loss surgery.

Let me explain more. In the beginning, after having weight loss surgery, your stomach organs become so small that even if you do not exercise, you will still lose weight. It is so small that even if you do not eat all the right things, just because you can't eat as much as you used to, you will lose weight. So even if you haven't fixed your self-esteem and learned to love yourself you will still lose weight. Which is great for many of us. It's great as long as we learn the right things to do along the journey. You have to learn the right things along the journey because one day, your stomach will expand. You may not ever be able to eat as much as you once did, but you will be able to eat enough to regain some weight. So, for those who never learned to eat in moderation, to focus on eating for survival vs. entertainment, to enjoy exercising, and to love themselves; a few years after the sleeve they are left to try to improve these things with a now expanded belly.

I am very much pro surgery for those with over 100 pounds to lose. Or for those who have really given it their all, but have not been successful. I just believe that more focus should be put on the maintenance routine vs. the pre-surgery requirements. Meaning, many doctors have patients for months or years go through pre-screening, the patient gets approved, but follow up care decreases after surgery. After the surgery is when the real work starts. I know for me mentally it was hard to get used to wanting to eat a full meal, but could only take a few bites. Therefore, I often ate to capacity. Also, with me having arthritis when it came to exercise, I was in pain, especially when walking. Ironically walking was the one thing that everyone suggested that I do. Most said walking was easy and very effective. Unfortunately, that was not the case. It was painful and often caused anxiety for me even months after losing some weight. I did not reach my goal weight after having the sleeve surgery. I was able to get down to 374 Pounds. Then, I got pregnant. Gained 20 pounds, then had a miscarriage in my second month. 3 months later I got pregnant again. I was able to successfully deliver Abram, but in this pregnancy, I put on 20 pounds more. Then post-baby, I gained 10 more pounds. I was 3 years out from my sleeve surgery and back up to 424 pounds. I was at a point in my life where I needed more than my sleeve to get the weight off me. It was then, I started to grow a love for exercise, it is now that I am praying for deliverance to eat better. So, I said all that to say, make sure you don't put all your eggs in one basket. God will send you different people to help at different times. However, your sole trust and faith should be in the Lord. Trust that he sends the right person, place, or thing at the right time.

Keep in mind that sometimes we have people that will help, and they are not sent to help. So, in the end, what might have been meant for help can turn out to be a hindrance. Your support person or tool should not be your all in all. At the end of the day, the person that is going to help you the most is the person that you see when you look into the mirror. You're going to have to help yourself by praying and using the almighty Spirit that is within you.

Bible verses to meditate on that will further help with this topic:

- It is better to take refuge in LORD Than to trust in princes. **Psalm 118:9**
- Stop regarding man, whose breath of life is in his nostrils; For why should he be esteemed? **Isaiah 2:22**
- Now the Egyptians are men and not God, and their horses are flesh and not Spirit; So, the LORD will stretch out His hand, and he who helps will stumble, and he who is helped will fall, and all of them will come to an end together. **Isaiah 31:3**
- Woe to those who go down to Egypt for help and rely on horses, and trust in chariots because they are many and in horsemen, because they are very strong, but they do not look to the Holy One of Israel, nor seek the LORD! **Isaiah 31:1**

Supporting Yourself

All of us have to encourage ourselves to really be successful at anything in life, but some of us will have no choice but to help ourselves. I totally understand, it is one thing to have the support and not rely on it 100% and another thing to want support, but it's not there. Both are not using the support system 100%. One is because he or she chooses not to and the other is because he or she has no one to help. So how do you move forward with absolutely no support? Unfortunately, you have to do just that. You move forward. Many of the obstacles you go through in life that really put your back up against the wall cause you to go through it alone. However, you are only alone if you are looking at it from a carnal standpoint.

No, you may not have a man or a woman to talk to and lead you through the way, but you have Christ. Many times, we are put into situations that we cannot count on mom, husband, bestie, or in between. For some situations, God wants you totally to be reliant on him. If this is your destiny journey, your influencers may not be able to give advice because they have not walked in your shoes. In this journey, you may even notice that you cannot even rely on yourself to know the answer.

It is also best to understand that support comes and goes. That your destiny helpers are only assigned for specific periods of the journey, then you have to keep it moving until the next arrives. Let's look at your journey as a journey on the city bus. You are you, and the bus is your help to make it to your destiny. On this route, you will find that only certain buses are en route to carry you down a particular street.

Sometimes your bus is traveling East and West waiting on you to get there, but because you are stuck standing at the South/North intersection, you keep missing it. If only you would step out on faith and walk alone for a block or two, you will arrive at this location. Your bus, this vehicle, this destiny helper is ready and waiting to help. Then, once you stand out on faith and you make it to this bus, keep in mind that this bus is only designed to carry you East and West. So, understand that this too will not get you all the way to your journey in most cases. After you have traveled some distance it's time to get off. It's time to take the support and help that you gathered and make your way to your next stop. Now, when you get off the bus it maybe others getting off too. Some may travel the route you take; some may go a path you have already taken. Perhaps you can point them in the right direction, but either way, as you direct them in their direction you must not revert back.

You must stay on your path and prepare to go to your next location. If you stop and stand still, you will find that life continues to move around you. You will find that instead of you reaching your destiny, you will hit a stagnation period. While you are stagnant, you may ask for help. Some may know, and some may not know. Some may even pretend that they know and if you follow them, you could be led off course. Often times, you will have to pull out your GPS, your bible, your prayer life, your internal navigator for help. With a set landmark and a focused path, you will eventually get there. Some faster than others, some fewer curves or fewer hills than others. But you will get there.

Bible verses to meditate on that will further help with this topic:

- Trust in the LORD with all your heart and lean not on your own understanding; in all your ways submit to him, and he will make your paths straight. **Proverbs 3:5-6**

- Look at the birds of the air; they do not sow or reap or store away in barns, and yet your heavenly Father feeds them. Are you not much more valuable than they? **Matthew 6:26**

I hope that you are encouraged, that you if need be, you can do this thing on your own. I want you to have support, but it's nothing like being mentally strong enough to do it by yourself if need be. So now that you understand that people will come and go, it is easy to receive help. It is easier to love on the people that will come to help. This way, once they reach their end session with you, you will be happy for the help that they did provide, rather than disappointed in the help that they did not offer. Nine times out of ten, where they stopped at was as far as they could carry you.

It's a big world outside

Support these days are everywhere, especially if you are technology savvy. In this case, support is a touch screen away. Here are just a few places in which you can find some help.

❖ Friends- How many friends/ associates do you have that don't really know that you want or need their help? Have you ever really reached out to these friends and had a conversation on how you could be of help to each other? Using the steps from Activity #15 will help create a proper dialogue to really set up an accountability partner.

❖ Family- This includes young and old. In-laws and blood. Many of us have children that would love to go on a unique vacation when mommy or daddy hit that specific goal. Let them help you. Be sure to use family members strength for help and to also be clear on what way you would like help.

❖ Church- Many of us go to church. Then, we run out of the doors as soon as the service is over. Lol, I'm often guilty of this. Try hanging around and building a relationship with some people that you share the same faith base with. Exchange phone numbers/social media contacts with members. You will find that many of you may have a lot of things in common. We often tend to have only a select few of people that we hang out with. For the most part, churches are continuously growing and getting new members. Be sure to also try to build a healthy relationship with some of the new members too.

❖ Gym- Now it may take strength to get you in the door by yourself. And, even though it feels like everyone is watching you when you go to the gym, most are not. Most people in the gym are on their grind and just notice that you use the equipment wrong lol. That's all. Yes, in life, we sometimes have haters that will give you an eye, but they are at the grocery store and everywhere else too. Are you no longer going to go anywhere? I also find that the classes at the gym are more friendly. After going for a while (if you have a welcoming smile) many people will talk to you and even notice when you are not there. Also, after class stick around, maybe go to the sauna or the locker room. People are there and ready to talk. Just be sure only to get yourself involved in the positive talk. You don't want to be associated with negativity.

❖ Meet-Up Groups- Search your local city for events. The parks and libraries often have free activities for all age groups. It makes it even more comfortable when you take the kids or grandkids to the events. Many adults sit in one general area while watching and waiting for the kids to enjoy the activity. Simply smile and say hello!

❖ Social Media- Billions of people are online at one time. Join different groups. Comment on people's posts. Make friends with some of your friend's friends. Don't become a stalker, just simply say hello, give a compliment and let them know that you are looking to make new friends. You will find that even though you are looking for someone to partner with for your fitness journey, that you may first bond on other commonalities. Maybe you both have a school-age child, or you both are breast cancer survivors, or you both recently saw the new movie that just came out. Concentrate on what you have in common.

Bible verse to meditate on that will further help with this topic:

• And though a man might prevail against one who is alone, two will withstand him—a threefold cord is not quickly broken. **Ecclesiastes 4:12**

"Surround Yourself with Positive People Who Believe in Your Dreams
Distance yourself from negative people who try to lower your motivation and decrease your ambition. Create space for positive people to come into your life.
Surround yourself with positive people who believe in your dreams, encourage your ideas, support your ambitions, and bring out the best in you."
— Roy T. Bennett, The Light in the Heart

FAB Activity #16/ Building Relationships

List 5 people or places you can go in which you can work on building a relationship… Keep in mind that at this time your sole purpose is to simply build a relationship. It's a bonus if that person later turns into a support/ accountability partner.

Example: Crystal at church. She is a lovely person, and on Facebook, it looks like she works out a lot. I could build a relationship with her. She and I could possibly work out sometimes together once we get to know each other.

1.

2.

3.

4.

5.

FAB

Chapter 6 Failure is not an Option!

You tried to diet and lose weight, but it did not go as planned. Is that considered a failure? Well, it depends on how you look at it. It's a failed plan, but not a failure for you. Just because your plan does not go as you planned, it does not make you the loser or the failure. You only fail or lose when you stop trying. Almost every great invention was created off trial and error. You try something, you receive an error, and you try again until you succeed.

If I had $1 for every time, I restarted my fitness journey I am sure that I would be a millionaire by now. I have tried so many things. Some, I tried and failed because it was not a great idea to start with such as when I tried the water only diet or the veggie-only diet. I enjoy eating and I also enjoy eating a variety of foods. If I struggle saying no to eating cookies occasionally, then How would I go for weeks saying no to everything? Not only was it challenging for me. It also was not healthy. Our body needs a balanced diet. We need to focus on making lifestyle changes, not quick fixes. Some diets I tried and failed because I wasn't consistent enough, such as me deciding to work out 5 times a day and eat 1800 calories. The diet was very well thought-out. It was healthy and doable, but I was not fully mentally prepared to stick with it. Some other diets I started and failed just because I was comparing my journey to someone else.

Well, this particular one that I compared myself in the beginning to others the most was not a diet. It was a drastic lifestyle change. It was when I had the Gastric Sleeve surgery in 2014. I've always been told the bigger you are, the faster you lose. So, you would think at 515 pounds that the weight would practically melt off after the surgery. Wrong... well at least wrong for me. You see when I had my surgery, I exchanged contact information with about 5 other ladies who also had their surgery that weekend. WE were "Surgiversary Sisters." Well, from time to time, we would inbox each other and ask how things are going. Everyone would share their numbers, and it always left me feeling unsuccessful. It wasn't that I was not losing any weight when we chatted. In fact, we were losing at the same speed. However, I was 200 pounds heavier than them. So, when they are 250 and lose 50, and I'm 480 and lose 50 it's not as much of a big deal. At 430, when I walked the streets, people still stared. When I got in my vehicle and tried to fit in the seatbelt, it still didn't fasten. When I got on some scales, it still said error. So, though I was losing just the same as them, I wasn't like them. In the beginning, I didn't get all the praise from onlookers, I wasn't 50 pounds away from my goal weight, I was not one pound away from "Onederland". I didn't feel as successful.

To make matters worse as I stated in the previous chapter, 2 years post-surgery, I became pregnant. I gained 20 pounds but later had a miscarriage. I was devastated. I lost a child in which my husband and I planned for, and I gained weight. That was a double whammy. 3 months later, not yet having lost the 20 pounds that I gained from the pregnancy, I got pregnant again. I had a perfect pregnancy. I delivered a happy, healthy, fussy, baby boy. Oh, I forgot to mention I gained 20 pounds with that pregnancy too. Not too bad considering with my oldest son, I gained 60 pounds during his pregnancy. That put me back up to 414 pounds and my sleeve allowed me to eat more than when I first got it. I tried to lose it but did not lose a pound. In fact, I gained and found myself back up to 424 pounds. So at that time I was very scared and embarrassed that I will get back up to 515 pounds. In fact, I had a family member tell me, "girl, you gained all that weight back". Talking about feeling like a failure. At the time, we were out to eat dinner, so you know how that ended. I ate out of stress. I ordered the wrong food (high carb pasta), overate, and cried about it later.

I thank God I didn't give up. Thank God that he put it in me to try again. In fact, it was in church that I was pushed to get back on my journey. My Pastor, Prophet Verna Du Pont (I love you, Pastor) told me that God said he was worried about me regarding my weight. She was very kind with her words but firm regarding the matter. That really hit hard with me. That my God, who is in control over everything, is worried about me. Dang, I must be doing pretty bad to worry God, is what I thought. The doctors may get worried, my family may get worried, I may get worried, but when my creator is saying he is worried this has now hit a new level. This was my push at that time to try harder. To be honest, I would try hard, and it seemed like some days I fell flat on my face. Many days, I still felt like I was 515 pounds. In all honesty, this is the reason I take so many pictures. Though I take a lot of pictures now, it was not always this way. My pictures are what allows me to compare and to really see how far I have come on my journey. So now, yes, even those pictures that I wouldn't dare put on social media. Those pics where I look like a blimp, I save those pics. I save those pics because I know that soon, I will be able to use it as a before and after photo. Though I may restart my journey over and over again, I am not a failure unless I quit trying.

FAB Activity #17/Take a look back

Sometimes, to move forward, we must look back at our history to avoid making the same mistakes. What have you tried in the past that did not work? List everything that you have tried. Next, write, Why did it not work. Be honest, did you give it enough time? Did you give it your all? Was it unrealistic to start off? Did you not properly prepare? If it did not fail, why did you stop?

What have you tried?

1.	
2.	
3.	
4.	
5.	

6.	
7.	

Bible verses to meditate on that will further help with this topic:

- I can do all this through him who gives me strength. **Philippians 4:13**
- But as for you, be strong and do not give up, for your work will be rewarded. **2 Chronicles 15:7**
- Have I not commanded you? Be strong and courageous. Do not be afraid; do not be discouraged, for the Lord, your God will be with you wherever you go." **Joshua 1:9**
- though he may stumble, he will not fall, for the Lord upholds him with his hand. **Psalm 37:24**

It comes with the territory

The sooner one can realize that you are on a Fitness Journey and not a race, the more likely he or she will be successful. In a race, you go as fast as you can. You don't stop. You don't look back and, in most cases, you know exactly where the finish line is. In a journey you will move forward, you will plan ahead, you will sometimes be hit with a detour, you may even find that you have to backtrack some steps. A lot of times with a journey, you have a set destination, but an estimated arrival time. You understand in your journey to leave cushion space for fluctuating traffic or detours. In your journey, you're only concerned with "your route" vs. in a race you are competing with society and is concerned with everyone's pace.

So, as you go along your journey you will find that you may hit some roadblocks (stalls), some detours (weight gain), and or bad weather (feeling down), but if you keep going, you will get there.

Stalls- Oftentimes, people feel like they are at the stall when the scale no longer moves. A true stall is when the scale does not move, and you also find that you are not losing inches.

Your body is now in maintenance mode. Your body has gotten used to the current activity that you are doing. Your body has adjusted to your caloric intake or to your activity level. At this time, you may need to decrease your calories or increase your activity. Also, if you were low carbs or low calories for months consistently, sometimes people find giving themselves 2-3 days of higher calorie intake is enough to confuse your body. What happens is after about 2 to 3 days your body knows to expect this higher calorie diet. Therefore, it intentionally prepares to burn more. Then on the 4th day, you go back to your lower calorie intake for a while, the body will still respond as if it is processing the higher calorie (Understanding that you may gain temporary water weight in the beginning). You may also need to do different types of workouts. The body is very intelligent. If you do 100 squats a day it will adapt, and you will no longer ache, you have gotten stronger, and now you must push further. This is why even though you work a job when you are walking all day, technically this does not count for exercise. Your body is used to your daily work. It needs that extra push.

Think about this… You have a Pro Basketball player. His/her job is to run back and forth continuously for several games a week. You would think if he runs for a living he does not need to exercise. False. You will find that they have an extra rigorous workout routine that they do very often to keep their bodies in shape and to push to higher limits. They just call it practice. As we call it a workout. Also, outside of practice… You will find that they do additional exercises and training. Remember a stall is temporary. It's your body resetting and adapting to your current activity. When trying to offset a stall, be sure that you are in a true stall. This means that you are not losing inches or pounds. If you find that the scale is not moving, but your clothes are getting smaller. YOU ARE NOT AT A STALL. Your body is transitioning. You are in fat-burning mode. Your unhealthy fat is turning into lean muscle. Lean muscle is what you want. Also, please know that lean muscle does not necessarily mean bodybuilder body. You can have muscle without being too muscular. Muscles are our friends. Muscle is what helps you burn fat even while you are sleeping. Again, MUSCLES ARE OUR FRIENDS.

- Weight gain- So during your journey, almost everyone goes through a period in which the scale goes back up. This can be very depressing to find that you are doing everything right, but the scale has gone up. Nine times out of ten if you are dieting and exercising and you experience a scale increase its water weight. You are not getting fatter. You are retaining water. Every pound on the scale is 3500 calories. More than likely, you did not eat an extra 3500 calories outside of your Basal Metabolic Rate (BMR).

Reasons we retain water: maybe you just recently started exercising more rigorously, maybe you just started increasing your water intake, maybe your hormones are shifting, or maybe you are under stress. It could be many different reasons, but this too shall pass. Always remember to weigh the same time every day (mornings are best), use the same scale, in the same location, with no clothing, or the same type of clothing. Know that the scale tells lies sometimes. The scale does not know the difference between fat, water, and muscle.

- Feeling down- We want to be thin, and we want to be thin now, and unfortunately, it does not happen like that. With that being said, we can sometimes find ourselves feeling down about our situation, and that's ok. Take this time to remember your why. Get upset and use this as your fuel to fight harder. Do not fall into a pity party focusing on what hurts or what you don't have. Focusing on what you do not have will not make you get it. Instead, focus on what you need to do to get whatever it is that you want.

Let's take this outside of weight loss. For some reason, when we go on a weight loss journey all the natural laws of obtaining goals, we try not to make them apply. A goal is a goal, and objectives are necessary to reach whatever it is. Let's shift the focus off of dieting. Our goal is to buy a Red Mazda 9 (lol I secretly want one!!!) You are not going to look outside your window every day to check and see if your Mazda 9 is out there. Lol. Stop getting on the scale so much. You are going to focus on what you need to do. Maybe you need to fix your credit, need to save some money, or you just need to actually find a dealer in your area. Either way, you need to shift your focus… You shift your focus from having the Mazda 9 to WHAT DO I HAVE TO DO to get the Mazda 9. Same thing with your fitness journey. Don't focus too much on the 50-pound goal. Focus more on WHAT DO I HAVE TO DO. Then once you do these things DAILY, you will obtain it. Notice I said DAILY.

We must be consistent with our journey. So, I totally know that we all have slipped up. A slip up is not the ruin to your journey. The ruin to your journey is when you allow that one slip up to turn into a week or a month of slip-ups. I know I've been there. I'm dieting, everything is going great, then BAM for whatever reason I fell off my journey. Maybe I did not exercise or I said, I was going to the movies and was not going to buy any popcorn. Then, when I get to the movies, not only do I buy the popcorn, I add extra butter. Now on the way home, I am upset with myself. Like dang, you said you were not going to eat it. Well, you done messed today up, you might as well enjoy the rest of the day… Sound familiar??? So now the next day I decide I want to get on the scale. Yup, as I thought I put on 3 pounds… It took me 3 weeks to lose those 3 pounds, and in 1 day I gained it all back (wrongggg… but this is how we feel) Now today I am in a funk. I'm too down to work out and to upset to care about what I eat. Matter of fact, at this point I don't even care if I lose weight… "Blank it" (lol all Christianity goes out the door at this point). I'm just gonna be fat. It's not meant to be. Big bones run in my family. The doctors want everybody skinny. I love myself just the way I am. Yadda yadda yadda... Now maybe a week, a month or 2 goes by and you are all over the board with your journey. Also, you probably put on more weight…

We have to stop this vicious cycle. It's not how hard you fall, but how fast you get back up. In that boxing ring you can get hit so hard you see Jesus when you hit the ground, but if you get back up the fight continues. On another hand, you can get hit with a power puff marshmallow hit. You hit the ground. If you do not get up. The fight is over... You lose!!! Get up, I say. Get up... Grab the ropes, pull on your opponent. I don't care what you have to do... but you got to get up. WE CAN DO THIS THING.

FAB Activity #18/ Understanding Calorie Counts

Ok, in order for you to take some priority off the scale you must really understand calorie intake. In this next exercise, I want you to think about that time that you were dieting and gained weight after having unauthorized food (lol, who makes it unauthorized). But anywho. You were doing great, and you slipped up, then you gained weight. How much did you gain? What did you eat? How many calories is it? Did you really gain fat?

Here is my example: I been going hard for a whole 2 weeks. I lost 5 pounds (mainly water) ... hey, the scale moved in the direction that I like. Sooooo I don't really care what I lost... I lost!!! Now I'm so hungry, and I decide to go grocery shopping... if no one has ever told you. Let me be the first to say it. Never go to the grocery store when you are hungry. You will buy everything... Throughout the store, I am very disciplined. In fact, I know the parameter of the store that has the healthiest food, so today that is the only place I'm shopping. Now it's time to check out. Low and behold the snickers bars are buy one, get one free. "Chileee I am so hungry, I been doing so good on my diet". Now you start to reward yourself with verbal praise to rationalize this purchase. "I have been drinking more water, I went to the gym 5 times this week, I haven't had no junk food in 2 weeks and I'm going to give the other snickers bar to the kids". So, you buy the snickers bar, and you ask the cashier to leave it to the side, because as soon as you get in the car... It's going down!!!. So, you eat your Snickers bar, and it was delicious. The next day for whatever reason you get on the scale, and you are 3 pounds heavier. All you can think about is that snickers bar. Now let me say if you went up 3 pounds... it's not a true gain nor all due to that snickers bar. Maybe you are near your menstrual cycle and that's why you are craving the chocolate from the first. Maybe you drank more water to make up from the Snickers bar, and your body has not released it. Maybe even after eating that Snickers bar, you decide you want to work it off, and you go extra hard in your workout, so your muscles out of protection begin to hold a little water. Now the next day you are 3 pounds heavier and because you did everything right it has to be the snickers bar right??? Wrong!!!! Let's look more into this.

Snickers Bar (standard Size): 250 Calories.
You gained 3 pounds. That's 3,500 X 3= 10,500 Calories

So, you would need to eat 42 Full-Size Snickers Bars to have gained these 3 pounds. Impossible!!! This does not even include the offset of the calories that you would've naturally burned at rest, making it room to eat about another 8 snickers bar on this day.

Let's look at your situation. The last time you went up on the scale (talking about over a 1-3 day span, not long term weight gain) How much did you gain? _____

How many calories does that equate to? (take the gained pounds and multiply by 3,500)

_____

What did you eat:

_____

How many calories was it? _____

How many would you have had to eat, to really have your increased on the scale? (take the calories gained and divide it by the calories in what you actually ate) _____

Did you eat that many????

More than likely, no… So, life goes on. The scale will go back down once your body adjusts. Keep doing the necessary steps that you have set up, and you will reach your goal.

Unrealistic Goals

Another reason why diet can sometimes not go as you planned is that your plan was all crazy to start off with. Some of us have so many goals, and we want to be able to reach them right away. I totally understand that when we have goals, they are set because we want them and the sooner, the better. However, most good things don't come easy or overnight. I know we all heard, it didn't come on overnight and it is not going to go off overnight. Though I too hate the reality… It is just that. It is a reality.

So, we find that when we set a goal, sometimes our goals are too hard or impossible to accomplish. Now, don't get me wrong your goals will stretch you. Your goals will push you out of your comfort zone. At the end of the day, one goal that works for one person may not work the same for you. So, when is your goal unrealistic? Many times, if you find that your short-term goal (meaning 1 day to 6 months) involve you doing something extreme, it's probably unrealistic. If your goal is to lose 30 pounds in 1 month and you have not lost 30 pounds in 1 year… That's kind of extreme. If your goal is to walk 5 miles a day and you have not walked 5 miles in one week that's kind of extreme. If your goal is to eat 20 carbs a day and your previous eating habits was primarily carbs that's kind of extreme.

Again, I am not saying that you can't go for the extreme or that you can't reach for the stars… because you can… Just give yourself a realistic time frame. Give yourself time to work up to this big goal. Let us take working out, for example. You want to walk 5 miles a day. Great for you! But right now, you currently walk 3 times a week for 1 mile. So, let's take that 5-mile goal, set it up as your long-term goal, but set smaller short-term goals in between. Maybe you will first walk 5 miles a week or maybe you will first increase your 1 mile 3 times a week to 2 miles 3 - 4 times a week. By setting your goals, smaller does not mean that you are an underachiever. The only way you are underachieving is if you intentionally sell yourself short. As you know, you have the time and ability to walk 3 miles a day, but you choose only to walk 2 miles a day. Now if you are selling yourself short. You have to think, Do you really want this goal? Let's examine your "why"... why is this a goal if your intent is not to stretch yourself. Let's look at a rubber band. It is made to stretch. It's built for it, it can take a pulling. However, every rubber band is different and can only use so much pulling at one time, or it will pop. Some rubber bands can even stretch further if you stretch them slower. You are that rubber band and a slight stretch is good, but overstretching can cause you to break. It can cause you to quit, it can cause you to give up. On the other hand, under stretching does not allow you to tap into its full potential.

Smaller goals build confidence. It takes more out of you to set a big goal and miss it versus to set a small goal and nail it. When you set small goals, and you accomplish them you should find that you grow more and more confident each time. Let's picture a boxing match. You are in the fight for your life (some of us literally). When you hit your opponent that's a step closer to the knockout. It probably also makes you feel more confident with each punch, but let's take that same fight. Your throwing punches, they are unmeasured, and you are missing most of them. Your confidence will automatically decrease, possibly causing you to quit. Not to mention that if you study boxing, you will learn that when a boxer throws a punch and misses, it takes more energy to recover versus when they hit the target. Next time you watch a match, look at the boxer. Look at when they throw an unmeasured punch, how they almost wrap that punch back around and have to fight to keep from even hitting themselves. That my friend is gravity for you. Once in motion, the faster you go, the harder it is to stop... So, I want you to look at it this way, the faster you accomplish a goal. The more confident you become, the harder it is to throw yourself off track. Now, someone just read this and automatically reverted back to saying yes... The faster I lose these 50 pounds is the better. NO! That's not what I am saying. Split the 50 pounds up... Answer me this, will you lose 5 pounds faster or lose 50 pounds faster? Of course, you lose 5 pounds faster. So, it's better to have short burst goals that you can accomplish faster versus attacking only the long goals.

FAB Activity #19/ Making your goals challenging

How to make a goal challenging without overdoing it: What goals can you set and accomplish over the next 7 days? Let's Challenge YOU just a little. Take whatever you did over the last 3 days and challenge it by 2. This will help you set a realistic challenge goal.

Example. You ate 100 Carbs every day for the last 3 days. Challenge yourself to eat 50 Carbs over the next 7 days.

Example: You said 2 affirmations to yourself every day for the last 3 days. Challenge yourself over the next 7 days to say 4 affirmations daily.

At the end of the day, you are reading this book because you want to lose weight or maybe you have a loved one that is trying to lose weight. So yes, the Long Term goal will be to lose X amount of pounds. However, when writing your goals I want you to focus on task-oriented goals. Remember the analogy with the penny? (In Chapter 1) You can see the penny on the ground and wish it was in your hands, but until you take action it will remain in that same spot. Well, it will remain as long as no one else comes to take it. That's a whole different story!

Create a 7 to 10 Day Challenge specialized to for you.

What behavior do you want to change or add into your journey?

_____

_____

_____

_____

What are you currently doing?

_____

_____

_____

_____

Multiply what you are currently doing by 2. What does that look like?

_____

_____

_____

Name
Challenge:_____

(Make it fun)

What are some tips/tricks to give yourself to help make sure you get it done?

1.	
2.	
3.	
4.	
5.	

Just when you thought the party was over. Remember that reward list that we completed in Chapter 2? It is now time to go back to it. How will you reward yourself during or at the end of the challenge? Maybe after day 1 reward yourself or maybe you want to wait till your done to reward yourself? Either way, pick a time frame and reward yourself.

Reward:

_____

_____

_____

_____

_____

_____

_____

_____

_____

Come back to this section after completing Challenge, if you find that you were not able to complete your challenge I need you to check 1 of 2 things. Was the goal realistic? Did you give it your all?

Explain_____

_____

_____

_____

_____

_____

_____

_____

Bible verse to meditate on that will further help with this topic:

- Be joyful in hope, patient in affliction, faithful in prayer. **Romans 12:12**

In between your failure – tree
And your triumph – tree,
The tree that is growing
Is known as your patience tree.
– Sri Chinmoy

A winner never quits, and a quitter never wins.

At the end of the day, no matter how many times you aim for your goals, just do not stop aiming until you reach them. Growing up in life, I think most of us read the story of the tortoise and the bunny. In this journey, you very well may be the tortoise. In fact, if you know the story, you know it is better to be the tortoise then the bunny... Lol, for anyone that is like what the heck is she talking about... Here you go....

It was a race. It was a 2 person/animal race. It was the great race of the Slow Tortoise against the Super-Fast Bunny. The race started, and as expected, the bunny took off. The bunny had so much momentum that he surpassed the tortoise with great measure. However, the tortoise stood his course. He moseyed along with the race. He kept his pace. Though it was slow, he did not stop. He did not look back. He did not doubt himself; he did not guilt himself for being slow. He just kept going. Now for whatever reason, the bunny who took off decided to stop for a break or two. Maybe he was tired. Maybe he just knew that the tortoise was moving so slow that he would never pass him. Either way, the tortoise continued his journey unbothered. He knew he either won first or second (AKA last) and that he was still going to finish. Long story short, the tortoise on his slow but consistent journey passed the bunny on his extreme and miscalculated race. The bunny rested so long that he did not see that the tortoise passed him by.

The tortoise won the race!!! My friend, you are a winner you can win. You will win! You just have to be in the race. The race of your life. So, there is no first or last place. It's death or life. Either your goals are going to fall dead or you are going to live your best life as you work towards your goal. Your goal may not go as planned. However, oftentimes in life, your setback is your come up. I reached a whopping 515 pounds, I have been able to experience this beautiful yet ugly journey. I have laughed and cried, and I'm not finished yet. As you read this book, I am a published Motivational Weight Loss Author. So, while some picked fun at me and belittled me at my 515 pounds. That very something that the enemy put out to destroy me is the very thing that has given me the success I have today.
Say it with me...' My setback is my come up" (now with a little more attitude and confidence). "My setback is my come up" and I want you to say this thing daily until you believe it! Faith it till you make it!

FAB Activity #20/ Faith it till you make it

Your mental exercise will be your most important exercise throughout your journey. Once you truly believe in you and your ability, you can do anything. So yes, we are doing affirmations again... We are "faithing" it until we make it. In this activity, create 3 affirmations that focus on how strong you are. That focus on how committed you are. That focus on how you will not quit.

Example: I am so happy, and I thank God that I am a go-getter. I accomplish all the desires of my heart. I know that my God would not place want in me that he does not give me the strength to receive.

1.	
2.	
3.	

Bible verse to meditate on that will further help with this topic:

- Therefore, since we have been justified through faith, we have peace with God through our Lord Jesus Christ, through whom we have gained access by faith into this grace in which we now stand. And we boast in the hope of the glory of God. Not only so, but we also glory in our sufferings, because we know that suffering produces perseverance; perseverance, character; and character, hope. And hope does not put us to shame, because God's love has been poured out into our hearts through the Holy Spirit, who has been given to us. **Romans 5:1-5**

The difference between perseverance and obstinacy is that one comes from a strong will, and the other from a strong won't. ~Henry Ward Beecher

The road to success is dotted with many tempting parking places. ~Author Unknown

Chapter 7 Whoop Whoop

If you follow me on my journey long enough at some point, you will hear me say, "Whoop Whoop." To some people, "Whoop Whoop" is a sarcastic way of saying big deal. For me, it's how I say You Rock!!! You did that thang. You are AWESOME! You can do this! Keep pushing! So how the heck did "Whoop Whoop", come about and what is it??? Shout out to my Friend, my Sister, my Business Partner, Curtis P Louis who helped me create it. Every time I wanted to celebrate someone on a Facebook post, I would reply" Whoop Whoop". Though I am writing a book, when it comes to commenting on a post, I am very simple and straight to the point. You will get an "Awesome", "You can do this", "We got this", "Yasssssss,", "I love you", or "Awwwww thank you". Lol, those are my go to's. So, when Curtis saw that for everything, and how I kept saying "Whoop Whoop", she was like, "I have to help you turn that into something". She did just that. It fits perfectly. It was meant to be. Now that she has helped me put meaning to my "Whoop Whoop", it means so much more to me and my FABS (Finding Acceptable Balance Sisters/Supporters).

In life, we all find moments when we either have to "Whoop Whoop". Or we did " Whoop Whoop", and that is how we accomplished our goals. Before I get more into the breakdown of " Whoop Whoop", I would like to tell a story about how important it is to "Whoop Whoop".

Many of you may have heard this story or a very similar one before, but here it goes. There was a young man driving in his car on a bright sunny day. Out of nowhere, the conditions rapidly changed. It began to storm. In this storm, it rained, hailed, lightened, and thundered. There was darkness all around him as he traveled on the highway. The rain was so heavy that even with the wiper blades on the highest speed, he barely could see ahead of him. He began to question his safety. The options he had were to push through, even with practically no sight ahead, to stop and wait out the storm, or to turn around and return home. The young man decided to turn on his high beams and to drive at a slower, but steady pace.

Within a few short miles, he was out of the storm. After making it through the storm, the sun shined bright again. He was back on his path to his destination. While traveling forward, he took a glance in the rearview mirror. He thought to himself, "The storm is over and was short-lived". To his surprise though, the storm was still going on in his rear. When he looked back, he also noticed that there were some cars pulled over in the storm. Though the young man was out of the storm, he began to think, "If only they would travel just a few more feet, they too would be out of the storm".

This story holds true for many of us. We are on the highway of life. Along this journey, sometimes we are traveling, setting goals, living life, and everything is beautiful - the sun shines bright! Our plans are going as we like or even better! Then Bam! Out of nowhere comes opposition. It begins to storm, and things are not as we planned. At this point, it is up to us to make a decision. Do we sit in the storm? Do we dismiss our trip altogether, or do we push forward through the storm? If you decide to push through the storm, you are "Whoop Whooping ", my friend!!!

Whoop Whoop

Willpower- the ability to control your own thoughts and behavior, especially in difficult situations.

Synonyms: self-control, self-discipline, determination, try-hard

Hope- to vision. The feeling that something desired can be owned or will happen

Synonyms: confidence, expectation, anticipation, courage

Optimistic- hopeful and confident about the future

Synonyms: positive, bright, cheerful, expectant

Oath- A promise

Synonym: pledge, word, assurance, vow

Perseverance- persistent in doing something despite difficulty or delay in achieving success.

Synonym: persistence, grit, resolution, determination

Looking further into Whoop Whoop

Willpower

The ability to control your own thoughts and behavior, especially in difficult situations. We all know that when we are on our fitness journey, willpower is key. Self-control is key. Many people think that the most important part of losing weight is to watch what you eat or to exercise. I disagree. Though they are very important and is a must, they are not the most important things. The most important thing is to make sure that your mind is strong and that you mentally believe in yourself and are willing to take the necessary steps to go on your fitness journey. Having willpower is the pushing force behind a person being able to go to a party and not eat birthday cake. Having willpower is the force behind a person being tired after work, but still going to the gym to workout. We all have so many things that occupy our time on a daily basis, that it is easy to get knocked off our fitness goals. Willpower will give you the force that is needed to make time for yourself.

Bible verses to meditate on that will further help with this topic:

- For God gave us a spirit not of fear but of power and love and self-control. **2 Timothy 1:7**
- Trust in the LORD and do good; so shalt thou dwell in the land, and verily thou shalt be fed. Delight thyself also in the LORD: and he shall give thee the desires of thine heart. Commit thy way unto the LORD; trust also in him; and he shall bring it to pass. - **Psalm 37:3-5**
- No discipline seems pleasant at the time, but painful. Later on, however, it produces a harvest of righteousness and peace for those who have been trained by it. Therefore, strengthen your feeble arms and weak knees. - **Hebrews 12:11-13**

"Willpower is the key to success. Successful people strive no matter what they feel by applying their will to overcome apathy, doubt, or fear." Dan Millman

Hope

The ability to visualize. The feeling that something can be desired. Many people fall short of their fitness goals before they even start. Many people start their goal off without even believing that they can achieve it. They simply throw out a number that they would like to see on the scale. However, the vision is missing. The vision of them one day being at their goal weight is not a reality. You are or will become what you imagine or meditate about on a daily basis. The problem with not having a vision, your purpose also lacks or runs in circles. Also, shallow vision does not create a mission. Clarissa, what are you saying? I am asking, "Why do you want to be 200 pounds? Why do you want to be 150 pounds? Why do you want to be whatever goal it is you are after"? Your reason why will form your vision. Still, don't believe me? Picture your ideal weight goal. How many pounds would you like to be? So now I snap my fingers, and when you get on the scale you are that very same number.

The only problem is you look and feel exactly how you look and feel today. Would that make you happy? Just because you're reading this book on being motivated to lose weight, 9 times out of 10, you will not! If you fail to focus on who you would like to become, you will not achieve it! Let me explain this more! My goal is to weight between 180 to 220 pounds approximately. Now is when the real vision starts! Now I must build this vision at this weight! I want to walk into any store and pick out any outfit and be able to fit it comfortably. I must see myself walking into these stores and buying clothing that at my goal weight, I can fit. To help visualize it, one may even go window shopping at these stores. Often times, when we go shopping, we only look at our current size.

Go look at the clothing in the size you desire to be!!! Look at how it's shaped to fit and feels. Take pictures with it up to your body. Vision yourself one day being able to wear it!!! If while holding this item you notice, fear, doubt, or disbelief, you have to work more on your vision and your beliefs that you have within. When you pick up that outfit that you want to get in, you should feel joy and excitement regarding the future. Think of it this way, you are going on vacation and your dream cruise cost you $1500. As you pay for your cruise, you become more and more excited, because even though you are not going on your cruise today, you know that the day is coming soon. It should be the same way with this outfit. Even though you cannot wear it today, you should feel excited that you will one day soon put it on because you are making payments now towards that dress. Not monetary payments, but you are eating healthy, exercising, and working on you in order to get to your goal. If you are not excited, either you don't really want it, or you don't believe in yourself! Either way, something must change!

Now, while visioning yourself at your goal weight don't only think about how you would look, or dress, also think about how you would feel. Will you feel happy? Will you be more confident? And most importantly, will you be bolder? How would you react and feel at your goal weight? Once you think about it, it's time to be about it. It's time to walk and act that way right now! A rich man will not act poorly until the day he becomes rich. If you do the things that the poor people do, you will forever remain poor. Instead, while you may lack money now, you are to do what the wealthy do. You are to learn to budget pennies. You are to read on how to invest. You are to save and carry yourself like a person with money.

If you wait until you have the money to play the role, either you will never get the money, or you will get the money, and you will soon lose it because you are not prepared to manage it. Therefore, you are to carry yourself now as the person at your goal weight. The confidence that you will have at that goal weight is something you are to develop now. Many people believe that when you loose weight your confidence will come. This is not 100% true. To be skinny does not mean that you are automatically confident. I am sure that you know or have heard of at least one thin person that lacks confidence. You are to practice having confidence now at this stage. Being confident in who you are today will give you the strength to be confident when you hit your goals.

Unfortunately, some people do not work on confidence, and by the grace of God, they still lose weight but don't notice it. They still do not feel pretty, or they become discouraged by the changes that their body has made. So, they find that they are at their goal weight, but still not happy. And yes, for many of us our body goes through changes with weight loss, and all are not good. Somethings sag a little more, and some of us get loose skin, etc. So be happy, be confident, be brave, be bold now!

So, we are visioning ourselves at our goal weight or size, we are mentally acting at our goal. What are some things that you would do if you were at your goal weight or size? I know for me I can't wait till I can take my son to go ride go-karts. I will be so excited to be able to climb in and out of the go-kart and to be able to fasten the seat belt. Excited to not have my stomach touch the steering wheel. So, I am thinking of trips and activities that I am looking forward to. Start thinking about the things you would do at that size. I know some of my friends, "Natalie and Alexis," will be so happy when they finally convince me to go jet skiing. I asked them "have you ever googled fat people getting on a jet ski"? Listen, it is not easy and seeing their failures was enough to scare me to not try it. Well, not until I build more upper body strength. It takes a lot of upper body strength to pull yourself out of the water and onto the jet ski. Now that I have released this into the atmosphere and this is a book about believing in yourself, I guess I now have to at least try to go jet skiing… Lol. Ok, guys give me one year to gain more upper body strength and get closer to my goal weight, then I am going jet ski riding!!! Let me set a goal date, we are currently in the summer of 2019. By the end of the summer of 2020, I promise I will have at least pushed my fears aside and tried to ride a jet ski. Jesussss be with me … LOL, but what is something that you really want to do and because you are not at your current size you can't or you are just hesitant for whatever reasons to try? Let's live life! Let's achieve our goals! Let's have hope that our future is bright and that we can do all things through Christ!

Bible verses to meditate on that will further help with this topic:

- May the God of hope fill you with all joy and peace as you trust in him, so that you may overflow with hope by the power of the Holy Spirit. **Romans 15:13**
- For I know the plans I have for you, declares the Lord, plans to prosper you and not to harm you, plans to give you hope and a future. **Jeremiah 29:11**
- But if we hope for what we do not yet have, we wait for it patiently. **Romans 8:25**
- Know also that wisdom is like honey for you: If you find it, there is a future hope for you, and your hope will not be cut off. **Proverbs 24:14**

When the world says, "Give up," Hope whispers, "Try it one more time." ~Author Unknown

FAB Activity #21/ Look at you! Look at you!

Write your vision of you at your goal weight. What will you wear, how will you do your hair, how will you feel, what will you do different?

_____

_____

_____

_____

_____

_____

_____

_____

_____

_____

_____

_____

_____

_____

Optimistic

To be HOPEFUL and CONFIDENT about the future. I like to say, focus on what you have and not on what you do not have. Look at the glass half full versus half empty. Life and death lie in the power of the tongue. Do you wake up daily and focus on what hurts or what shortcomings you have, or do you wake up thankful for what you have? Do you start your day ready to use and grow what you currently have, or are you held back because your focus is on what you do not have? Your focus and your outlook on life make all the difference in you obtaining your goals. In general, you will have whatever you focus on, whether it be good or bad.

Let's take a look at Matthew 25:15- 30

15 To one, he gave five bags of gold, to another two bags, and to another one bag, [a] each according to his ability. Then he went on his journey. 16 The man who had received five bags of gold went at once and put his money to work and gained five bags more. 17 So also, the one with two bags of gold gained two more. 18 But the man who had received one bag went off, dug a hole in the ground and hid his master's money.

19 "After a long time the master of those servants returned and settled accounts with them. 20 The man who had received five bags of gold brought the other five. 'Master,' he said, 'you entrusted me with five bags of gold. See, I have gained five more.'

21 "His master replied, 'Well done, good and faithful servant! You have been faithful with a few things; I will put you in charge of many things. Come and share your master's happiness!'

22 "The man with two bags of gold also came. 'Master,' he said, 'you entrusted me with two bags of gold; see, I have gained two more.'

23 "His master replied, 'Well done, good and faithful servant! You have been faithful with a few things; I will put you in charge of many things. Come and share your master's happiness!'

24 "Then the man who had received one bag of gold came. 'Master,' he said, 'I knew that you are a hard man, harvesting where you have not sown and gathering where you have not scattered seed. 25 So I was afraid and went out and hid your gold in the ground. See, here is what belongs to you.'

26 "His master replied, 'You wicked, lazy servant! So, you knew that I harvest where I have not sown and gather where I have not scattered seed? 27 Well then, you should have put my money on deposit with the bankers, so that when I returned, I would have received it back with interest.

28 "'So take the bag of gold from him and give it to the one who has ten bags. 29 For whoever has will be given more, and they will have an abundance. Whoever does not have, even what they have will be taken from them. 30 And throw that worthless servant outside, into the darkness, where there will be weeping and gnashing of teeth.'

Wow, that's deep. Now someone is reading and saying yes, the things the Lord trust me with are the things I must use and multiply. However, when you think of things you think of money, food, jobs, etc. Is your health not a gift from God? Is the enemy not plotting all day to steal, kill, and destroy everything about you? What blessings are you hiding because you are focusing on what you do not have?

Let's look at this parable this way…

To one he gave disease-free body, some money to buy food, a home to work out in and rest, a solid mind to function, friends/family for support. Let's stop right here… Because most of us have these 5, the problem is that we are looking at the condition of these 5 instead of seeing the blessings. He did not speak on the plowing or the sewing that the man who had 5 had to do. I am sure that he had to work hard to make his next 5. He merely talked on the end result. Many of us want the end result but don't want to do the work that needs to be done in between.

So maybe you are disease-free, but you have joint discomfort. At the end of the day, God still gave you more than he gave someone else. What are you going to do with it?

Maybe you have a job, but when you do your budget, you don't have much left to buy all the things you want. Let's still focus on you having something that another person doesn't have. Maybe God is waiting to see you properly manage this job cheerfully before he can bless you with a promotion? "We all know 2 Corinthians 9:7, right?

Each of you should give what you have decided in your heart to give, not reluctantly or under compulsion, for God loves a cheerful giver. **Corinthians 9:7**

When looking around, you may see things that you are not happy with and you would like to change about yourself. I have been there. I have had a home that I disliked returning to because of the condition that it was in, but if I'm totally honest the condition that it was in had a lot to do with me. The people I decided to let in, the way I mismanaged money and couldn't buy better furniture, and the way I lacked to clean caused bugs to appear. When I first moved into that very same house, I called it home. So, to be very honest, that home I was reluctant to come home to was in that condition because of the choices that I made or did not make. Either way, I still had a home. I still passed people on a daily basis who were sleeping at the park or bus stop. So maybe I did not have the money for a gym membership, but I did have access to YouTube and a front room with just enough space to do whatever I put my heart to do.

Now let's look at a solid mind. You may have some anxiety or occasional depression, but you have a fully functioning brain. You know right from wrong, day from night, you know how to seek spiritual or medical help if need be. So, do you seek help to grow your shortcomings, or do you dig a hole and bury the mental treasures that you do have?

Yes, friends and family's support come and go. Sometimes they help and sometimes they don't. Sometimes you give your all, and when you look back, they are nowhere to be found. You can't get water from an empty well. Some of us are standing at wells and keep lowering down buckets asking for water, but when the bucket returns empty, then we are upset. We are like, but I cut the grass around you, but I gave you this new pretty bucket for people to pull from you, but I managed your rope and made sure it had no slashes. God and the well, thank you very much for what you did from your heart while expecting nothing in return, but unfortunately, at this time you have done so much for the well, though it seems that it should be in the right position to help you. Though it looks as if it has water to give... It is empty. This well is dry and though you have done so much for it, at this moment what it has is not suitable for you. Yes, you may have seen it bring up some water for someone else, but maybe this well is not the intended well that God wants you to receive water from.

Bible verses to meditate on that will further help with this topic.

- and my God will meet all your needs according to the riches of his glory in Christ Jesus. **Philippians 4: 19**
- and we know that for those who love God, all things work together for good, for those who are called according to his purpose. **Romans 8:28**

So, let's make sure we are asking the right people for help. Lets not just ask because I have done for you before, or because I feel comfortable enough to ask you. God has a plan for us, and everything is about timing. Maybe it's a reason he won't let cousin Sheila help you and while you think she is being disloyal, God is protecting or molding you for something better.

Bible verses to meditate on that will further help with this topic.

- When you ask, you do not receive, because you ask with wrong motives, that you may spend what you get on your pleasures. **James 4: 3**
- "Be still before the Lord and wait patiently for him; do not fret when men succeed in their ways, when they carry out their wicked schemes." **Psalm 37:7**
- "God loves you and has a wonderful plan for your life!" **Lamentations 3:16**

Looking unto others

So there comes a time when we look at others' and their lives, and we may say, "God, you gave them more than you gave me. They have life easier than me. I have so much pain and hurt. Why me, Lord?" Let's make sure we look at each situation with an optimistic eye. Let's be happy for what we do have. This very well may be the very one thing that's keeping us from having more. This lack that you're going through maybe your very testimony, but you too focused on how things are not going you don't hear God's voice to know your next step to success. Maybe God is saying and pointing "LOOK! I gave her a healthy heart, I gave her a solid mind, I gave her full mobility, but all she can focus on is the joint discomfort.

Don't be like the man whom he gave one. Don't be a man or woman of God that digs a hole and hides the treasures that he does give simply because you are looking at what others have, or because you are looking at what you have and would like more. Be optimistic about what you do have, and in the right timing along with faith, your situation will change.

Bible verse to meditate on that will further help with this topic:

- Do not be anxious about anything, but in everything, by prayer and petition, with thanksgiving, present your requests to God. **- Philippians 4:6**

- I pray that the eyes of your heart may be enlightened in order that you may know the hope to which he has called you, the riches of his glorious inheritance in his holy people. **Ephesians 1:18**

Oath

To make a promise to oneself. In life, we make vows to others, and we give our all to keep it. However, when it comes to us, we are not as faithful. If the children or someone of love/respect, ask us to do something we sacrifice to make sure we do it. For others, we will call out from work. We will skip meals. We will go the distance, but when it comes to ourselves it is not the same. Especially when it comes to our health goals. It's like when it comes to taking care of our temple, everything else comes first. The crazy thing is we only get one body, and we must take care of it, or we will not be around to take care of anyone else. To put oneself first is not a greedy or rude thing. However, to not take care of the temple, GOD has created is a sin.

As Christians, we are designed to be fruitful and to multiply by adding the lost to the kingdom. How can we add the lost if we are lost? Yes, this is a weight loss journey, but many times it is way deeper than just that. To love anything more than we love God is a sin. Food addiction is a sin. The great thing is that God is not sitting high and condemning you. He is looking low and saying my poor child needs help. My child lacks a good quality of life. I want her to have more, but she puts everything else first.

Obesity carries many health conditions that could have been avoided. While God is saving you from High Blood Pressure, that time and resources could be put towards something else. If you get your eating under control, maybe more blessings can flow into your marriage. Yes, God is our all and all. God can do anything, but God is also a man of order. He will not take you to point D if you are still stuck at point B. Many times, there are things that we learn along our journey that helps us for the next testimony.

Bible verse to meditate on that will further help with this topic:

- Greater is he that is in you, than he that is in the world. **1 John 4:4**
- God is not a man, so he does not lie. He is not human, so he does not change his mind. Has he ever spoken and failed to act? Has he ever promised and not carried it through? **Number 23:19**

The truth is the truth

To make a promise and not keep it is a lie. It is still a lie even if it is a promise to yourself. This section, as I write it. I'm like, "man… This is tough wording God". In this particular section, I was woken up from out of my sleep to come and write. In no other section has this happened to me. I hope this message applies to you, just as much as it applies to me. As at this time, I am merely a vessel that God is using to speak to people. We have to do better with our health. God is not going to place a desire in us to do what we are not able to fulfill. We need to stop going at this thing with a carnal mind and use him to break these chains that we have holding us down.

This thing is bigger than just numbers on a scale for many of us. Some of us due to obesity are isolating ourselves. How can you speak and save a soul if you are in isolation? If you are in your home and don't leave much. Don't fellowship much, don't live this one life that you were given to live, who can you save? Many of us face depression due to being overweight. Many of us have dimmed lights. We are going through so much due to this health condition, and he just wants us to be free, but it takes a committed person. It takes fasting, praying, and seeking the face of God to get this weight off. We fast and we pray for houses and cars, but what about this temple that we only get one of?

What about this temple that once this heart stops ticking, that's it? Many of us can and will be freed from obesity; we just have to honor our promises to ourselves. We have to put more value on this beautiful body that God has made. We must make time to put ourselves first. That means we must work out, even when we have had a long day at work. We must still find time for it. How many times have you been tired after work, but because you made a promise to someone, you still went and did what you said you would do??? What about yourself? We must eat healthily. We must think healthy. We must try harder to keep our promise. We must lean unto to him.

Bible verses to meditate on that will further help with this topic:

- Trust in the LORD with all your heart and lean not on your own understanding. **Proverbs 3:5**
- I am the way and the truth and the life. **John 14:6**

FAB Activity #22/ Write an oath to not give up on yourself

What promises do you make to yourself?

_____

_____

_____

_____

_____

_____

_____

_____

_____

_____

_____

_____

_____

Perseverance

Perseverance- persistent in doing something despite difficulty or delay in achieving success.

Are you ready to fight? ARE YOU READYYYYYYY? It's time to strap up our boots and lace our gloves and get ready to fight. Get ready to push when we don't have any push left in us. To look at this thing and say…

"No matter what I am not going to give up. When others stop going, I am going to keep going. When opposition comes up against me, I am going to push back. I am not going to give up. Greater is he that is in me. I can do all things through Christ that strengthens me. I am more than a conquer. I am the head and not the tail. The Lord is my rock and my salvation, whom should I fear? I am fearfully made and bought with a price. He died on the cross so I can be set free from all my sins. He takes away my iniquities. Yay though I walk through the valley of death, I fear no evil. He made me in his own image. He cherishes me. He takes care of the birds and the fails. He will take care of me".

Read this, write this daily… until you believe it…

Affirmations in the Bible:

1. 1 John 4:4~ Ye are of God, little children, and have overcome them: because greater is he that is in you than he that is in the world.

2. Philippians 4:13~I can do all things through Christ which strengthens me.

3. Romans 8:37 ~ No, in all these things we are more than conquerors through him who loved us.

4. Deuteronomy 28:13~The LORD will make you the head, not the tail. If you pay attention to the commands of the LORD your God that I give you this day and carefully follow them, you will always be at the top, never at the bottom.

5. Psalm 62:2~ He alone is my rock and my salvation, my fortress where I will never be shaken.

6. Psalm 139:14 ~I praise you because I am fearfully and wonderfully made; your works are wonderful, I know that full well.

7. 1 Corinthians 6:20~ you were bought at a price. Therefore honor God with your bodies.

8. 1 Peter 2:24~ "He himself bore our sins" in his body on the cross, so that we might die to sins and live for righteousness; "by his wounds, you have been healed."

9. Psalm 103:3~ He forgives all my sins and heals all my diseases.

10. Psalm 23:4~ Even though I walk through the darkest valley, I will fear no evil, for you are with me; your rod and your staff, they comfort me.

Bible verses to meditate on that will further help with this topic:

- Then God said, "Let Us make man in Our image, according to Our likeness; and let them rule over the fish of the sea and over the birds of the sky and over the cattle and over all the earth, and over every creeping thing that creeps on the earth." God created man in His own image, in the image of God He created him; male and female He created them. **Genesis 1:26-27**
- For God so loved the world that he gave his one and only son, that whoever believes in him shall not perish but have eternal life. **John 3:16**

- Look at the birds of the air; they do not sow or reap or store away in barns, and yet your heavenly Father feeds them. Are you not much more valuable than they? **Matthew 6:26**
- And my God will meet all your needs according to the riches of his glory in Christ Jesus. **Philippians 4:19**

Chapter 8 From past to Present!

It ain't Ova… In my Kirk Franklin voice. I am not at my goal weight, but even if I was life has just begun. I am a new me. I have a second shot at life. At the start of this book, I talked about my final breaking point. Though that was my final breaking point, it was so many breaking points that occurred before that one. I know it can feel like an eternity getting this weight off. I know we can often feel like we can't take any more, but yet we are not ready to fight. Oh, how I know this feeling so well. At my highest of 515 pounds, I felt like I was imprisoned in my own body. I felt like I was in a cage. I felt like mentally I wanted to do so much, but I was held captive by my own body. To be honest, I felt like I was going to die if I did not get the weight off. So drastic measure sometimes takes drastic actions. Which is why I had the gastric sleeve surgery done. On top of the drastic step to make matters even more drastic I went to Mexico to have the surgery. I chose to go to Mexico after not getting insurance coverage here in the United States.

I tried to get coverage for the surgery but seems like I was just shot down every turn I took. I remember right before getting pregnant with my oldest son, (who is now 10 years old) I tried to get the gastric sleeve. I was going to the doctor for approval. I was setting up the necessary appointments. I was 413 pounds and only 22 years of age; at this time, I thought I had more mobility and endurance. While I was going through the process of getting the surgery, my insurance changed, and the company picked up stricter bariatric surgery guidelines. At this point, bariatric surgery was considered cosmetic surgery. I was 413 pounds. There was nothing cosmetic about me having the surgery, it was life or death. The surgery was very much needed. At that time, I had no high blood pressure, diabetes, sleep apnea, or any of the other common things that sometimes come with being obese. In fact, at this time, I barely had arthritis. As I type this, I'm like man, if they would have helped me during this time I probably would have better mobility with my legs and go through less joint pain, but on the other hand, I do understand that all things work for my good. I do understand that had I lost the weight at that stage in my life my story would not be the same. So deep down inside, I'm ok with it.

So back to when I was 413 pounds and NOT out of shape... So, I thought... A year after having my son I hit another time that should've been my breaking point... I remember going on a girl's trip with some college friends. I was so excited to meet back up with them, and they were excited to meet with me. In my freshmen year lol I would like to have called myself the life of the party. Not the center of the party, but the life of the party. So, I'm sure when we all met up only four years later, they were expecting to meet the same, Rissa. Hell, I thought I was the same, Rissa. It was this trip that showed me how much of life I was missing out on. Instead of me having a great time, I left this girls trip feeling embarrassed. At the ripe age of 24, we were trying to live our best life in one weekend, but I just could not hang. I needed to sit every few minutes. I needed to know how far we were walking before we would walk. I became the center of attention, but not in a good way. I was the needy friend that they had to cater to from lack of endurance. I will hear, "Rissa will you be able to walk? Rissa are you ok? I don't know if we should go there, it's a lot of standing". I then felt bad because I was also holding them back from enjoying their trip. Though no one said anything, the sympathy showed said enough. I was 24 and unhealthy.

You would think that it would have sunk in by now and I would have gone home and said: "enough is enough I have to get this weight off me". And your right! I did. I went home, and I started a workout and diet. It seems as though I've started working out and dieting all of my life repeatedly, but still I reached 515 pounds. By this time, I met my then-boyfriend, now-husband Angelo. Again, I found myself in a very similar situation in which I was the one that could not keep up. After hitting my breaking point, again and again, I decided to have the Gastric Sleeve Surgery, and I was going to Mexico to do so. Almost everyone I told what I was going to do was against it. Yes, it was a scary time for me, but not as scary as thinking that I would die and leave behind my child. Or not as scary as thinking that my child would live a life and that I would not be included because I was too out of shape to keep up. I had to do something. I had to change the quality of my life, and I did just that. With all my nerves, fears, and limited support, I made the best decision of my life. I had the Gastric Sleeve Surgery. It was not a walk in the park, but I did it.

How was having gastric sleeve surgery in Mexico

Many people ask how was it going to Mexico for surgery? I guess it was no scarier than doing it right here in the United States. The things that shook me or made me nervous would have been the same no matter where I had it. I received all different types of rebuttals from why I should not go to Mexico to have the surgery. Never let someone that has not been through the same situation be the main factor as to why you do not move forward. I do believe, most who were against me going to Mexico had my best interest at heart… In fact, that's why they were so afraid for me to go. However, facts are facts! They did not know how it truly was, so they could not really give advice. They were just reacting off fears for me.

Common Reasons why people said I should not go to Mexico:

Language Barrier: They said, it's a different country and they are not going to speak English. You will not understand them. Yes, it was a new country with Spanish as the primary language. Nope, I don't speak any Spanish. Lol. However, my Surgeon spoke great English. If I remember correctly, he even had some training here in the States. The nurses that were assigned to me spoke English. The Transportation staff and Hotel staff spoke English. Now when I voluntary went out to the market to shop not everyone spoke English, but many did. Hubby even got a tattoo while we were in Mexico. Before my life is over, I plan to visit many places that English is not their primary language; this will not be my deal-breaker!

Too Dangerous: Some family members mentioned the crime rates and how dangerous it may be. Listen! Just think about it. What place on earth can you travel to and they do not have an unsafe tourist location? Hell, I'm from Detroit, Michigan. At one point, it had the highest crime rate in all of the United States. I made it out ok. Besides the facts, my tour guide advised us of all the areas not to visit.

It's not going to be clean: They were worried about the sanitation of the hospital. When I got there, it was very clean. In fact, the people treated me better than the care I get here in the United States. The staff was nice, and they came around and checked on me. When I entered my room, I noticed it was a glove (not sure if used or not) on the floor. I mentioned it and it was immediately taken care of. Additional staff came in to apologize and everything. I felt bad afterward because I know someone got in trouble about the glove being on the floor. Other than the glove on the floor, I didn't see any sanitation hazards and because this planted fear tainted me. TRUST… I was looking.

I mean those were the main reasons why people said I should not go. I probably could have come up with a few more reasons as to why I shouldn't have gone. I knew what was more important. I was 515 pounds and fighting for my life. In life, whenever we do something, you will find reasons as to why things will challenge you or take you outside of your comfort zone. Please know opposition DOES NOT warrant a reason for acquittal. To be honest, I am happy I went to Mexico, but at the same time, it makes me angry as an American Citizen. I am born and raised here in this Country. I have worked since the age of 15 years old and paid my taxes. All my adult years, I've had Medical Insurance (besides a short lapse this year). My point is, why did I have to go to another country to have surgery? I feel like the United States has failed me. Yes, I ate the food, and I got up to 515 pounds, but I've been screaming for help all my life. It seems like all I ever got was judged and told to stop eating, but not much help other than that. When I spoke to my primary doctor, he sent me to a nutritionist; whom then sent me to a therapist. Running into circles paying everyone for their services, not getting proper help, but steadily getting fatter. For instance, my right leg was not always bowed. The extra weight made my leg bow. In my mind, all I can think of is all the help I screamed for and no one could help me. Something should've helped. I asked for weight loss pills and I was denied. I went to the doctor looking for health tips for losing weight; they would at times say wait lets focus on XYZ first. In my head, I'm thinking, "I came in because I need help with my weight.

My joint pain, my depression, or whatever else at this time can wait. I want the weight off, and the rest will get better". Yes, lol I am still in my feelings about it. Not just for me, but for every other person that is fighting the same journey without proper help. To be honest, this is my main hesitation for going to get a sleeve revision. I know at this point if I go get a revision it will shatter the hope of others like me that are trying and can't get the procedure done. We can lose this weight without surgery. It will be a challenge, but it can be done. This takes me back to when the doctors would show me charts that said at my weight of 515 pounds I only had a 2% chance of being able to lose the weight without the surgery. So, it was like a double slap. We can't give you the surgery and here is a paper saying you can't do it without the surgery. That is bologna! With my God, all things are possible. Yes, the surgery did help me a lot, but now it is God fighting this fight for me. If I had the fight I have today five years ago; I would not have needed the surgery. So, to anyone out there trying to lose weight, you can do it with or without surgery. You must fight all while getting knocked down! Believe in God and you'll never get knocked out!!!

Returning home and after the surgery (chicken wing)

For me, the toughest aspect of having surgery was the mental process. I had to get used to wanting to eat a large portion, but getting full after a few bites in. I did not tell a lot of people about my surgery for about two years. I guess for me; I did not go public for fear of people judging me or for fear of it not working. I was a very slow loser. It took me two years to lose 130 pounds. When I decided to tell people, I've had the surgery my tool was not working the same. I had already regained 50 pounds. At that point, I felt like my tool no longer worked. I guess being able to get the weight off again after knowing my tool was not working the same gave me a certain confidence. I also told people to let them know that the sleeve is not a fix-all procedure for most of us. It's a tool just like they say. It's a tool that you must use correctly because if used improperly… overeating past full will stretch your tool out, and you will find yourself rising again on the scale.

Those who recently had the sleeve or never had the sleeve may ask how you regained the weight. I did get pregnant two years from my sleeve, and that had a big effect, but to be honest, Rissa went back to her old eating habit's. Many women, after losing weight, find it easier to get pregnant. My first pregnancy was intended. The doctors informed us that after two years post-surgery that my body would have healed enough to manage pregnancy. We waited two years and within about 3 to 6 months of trying to get pregnant, it happened. My husband and I were so happy. However, I was scared and I was exercising but picking up weight fast in this pregnancy. Sadly, to say less than two months into this pregnancy, I miscarried. Another whammy added to that is I gained 20 pounds during this short time frame. Being a little disappointed and thrown off track, I did not jump right back into a fitness routine or healthy eating lifestyle.

By the grace of God without trying three months later, we were pregnant again. This pregnancy I did carry full term. Though I was very high risk, so much that 4 to 5 high-risk doctors after reading my chart refused to provide me with prenatal care. I did eventually find a doctor and I did have a successful pregnancy. No complications and was blessed with a beautiful, very active little boy. I forgot to mention that I gained 20 more pounds in this pregnancy. Which to me was not that bad. 20 pounds in 7 weeks vs. 20 pounds in 38 weeks is way more acceptable. Of course, I had the baby, and I jumped right into my fitness plan. I had lost almost 10 pounds within a month after having him. I was back on my trip to skinny. LOL... Well, I don't desire to be "skinny," but you know what I mean. To be honest, where it fell back apart, I have no clue.

One day I was dieting and exercising the next day I was at 424 pounds. I was 10 pounds heavier than my post-pregnancy weight. So, this was a reality check for me. Never in a million years did I think that I was going to have the sleeve than regain the weight. I get inboxes from people all the time that says that they have gained all or most of their bariatric surgery weight back. To be honest it's so many people, that I think we need to go back and look at the playbook on these surgeries. I know for many they jump through 1000 hoops to get approved. Then afterward, the care simmers down. Not sure if it's because the patient does not go as much or it is because the doctor does not require it. However, the real work happens after the surgery; the mental and physical work.

Let me explain, have you ever studied so hard right before your test, take the test, pass the test, but months later someone asks you a question and you can't remember the material? It seems like it's the same thing with this surgery. We do everything to get approved. Say whatever we need to say to make sure we get the surgery. Try whatever crazy diet we can to get the surgery. Receive all kinds of counseling and such. Get the surgery, then we "Skinny" and feeling ourselves, and a lot of the things we were doing before ceases. The encounters that we were having with the doctors stop or slow down too. Then for some the weight returns.

People often ask do I have any regrets, or would I recommend the sleeve? I have no regrets. The sleeve saved my life. I do wish I had proper follow-up care. Maybe that would have made a difference in me stretching my sleeve or maybe not. I am blessed that I do not have any big life-changing complications that some people do face after having the sleeve. The only complication I picked up is acid reflux, which they did inform me that I would have. However, it was only supposed to be for a year or two. I am 5 years out and get terrible acid reflux if I do not take my medication daily. That too is a little scary because prolonged use of omeprazole is not healthy either. Please know, I would take the acid reflux over the pain and isolation, I felt at 515 pounds any day.

I am very happy to say currently, I am at my lowest weight since High School. I am now down to 345 pounds leaving me at 170 pounds loss. Whoop Whoop! This is only the beginning. My goal is to get to 180 to 220 pounds. To be honest, I have no clue what number I would like to get to. I know I want to feel free and light. I want to be able to shop at any store. I want to be able to run and bend freely. I want to live my best life, and I can't necessarily pin a number to that. With that being said, I have also been overweight all my life. So, I have no idea what size will look good on me. Now, I also understand body composition. I know that you can have two people that weighs 200 pounds and one will look leaner than the other because of muscle mass. So that's what I am working on. I am working on losing weight and leaning up. I am currently on a product that I have been on for the last year that helps with that. I call it Liquid Lipo.

I take one spoon daily, and it has really been able to help me shrink my fat cells, block my fat absorption, and curb my appetite. LOL, in other words... LOSE THIS WEIGHT. Currently, I am a distributor, and I do sell this product. I have tried many things, but this has been the first thing that I have seen lasting results. Now to be fair, I would also like to say that this is the first thing that I have ever stuck too. The system is very simple to follow and allows me to fit it into my lifestyle. Not the other way around. At the end of the book, I do offer a discount link where you can feel free to give the product a try.

No longer just about me

Living out my journey, I have found my purpose for life. In my heart of hearts, I believe that my whole purpose of walking this earth is to motivate people along this journey. To motivate people to love themselves and to believe in God along the journey. To understand that this is not a quick fix but a journey. To help people learn to enjoy the journey and not rush through life. We only get one life and living Friday to Friday makes us miss out on so much.

I also have my children that are looking up to me. Looking for me to be healthy for them. I am also setting an example to let them know that you can do whatever you set your mind to do. Starting up my business has not been an easy task. All my life, I lived a point A to point B type of life. Meaning, I knew what the next step was before I took the last step; for the most part. With me growing FAB, I am at a point where I don't have any mentor that I can reach out to and say hey… what's my next step in growing my FAB Business? How did I do on that last step? Well, not unless I'm paying for the advice. Lol. Yes, I know nothing in life is free, but I also know that everyone help is the right help. So being that this is my journey and God's plan only he really can guide me and lead people in my life to give me my next move. I am praying that God helps me to align my timing upright for me to hear exactly what I am going to do next.

Now, I will say that I have been sent different individuals that help with certain tasks, such as Chanel, Curtis, Michelle, just to name a few. However, God is my all-inclusive help. Let me explain:

Let's take getting your bachelor's degree as an example. When you go to school, you have Professors. Each professor is assigned to a certain course. That professor is only skilled to help you with that one course. Though you have 50 courses to take, the Professor is only skilled to help with that one course. Now because he is qualified to help, you will do great at that course…. The problem is… do you really need this course? What are you majoring in? Are you majoring in mathematics, but you are taking a drama class? That's when a Guidance Counselor comes into place. The Guidance Counselor will look at the bigger picture. The Guidance Counselor is looking at the end project and will give you a set outline of what and when to do it.

My God is my Guidance Counselor. The bitter/sweet truth is he will not put more on you than you can bear. So, he will not promote or show you your next level before you can handle the current level. As I go along my journey, it is his plan and not Rissa's. So many people ask me, Clarissa, what is in the future? To be honest, in my spirit, I feel it will be great. I'm just waiting to see what magnitude of great. As I write this, we are 5 Months into 2019. In January of 2019, I did not know that by the end of 2019, I would be a Published Author. At the beginning of 2018, I did not know that by the end of 2018, I would be a Full-time Entrepreneur. So much is changing in such a little time. I am just riding along my journey, seeking my God, better health, and trying to help others along the way.

At the end of the day, this is what life is about. It is about helping others, and unfortunately, this is rare these days. I remember earlier this year; I decided that a treat to myself would be to give 5 Flowers to 5 Random women. Boy oh Boy, it was hard to pass out the flowers. Everyone wanted to know why? Why was I doing something nice? What did I want in return? It was not an easy task to convenience the ladies that I was simply trying to give back to the universe. This, my friend, is very sad. They had such a hard time accepting this gift because it is a rare occasion for a human to help humans with no motives.

FAB Activity #22/ Give to receive Joy

This is the last activity in this book. I want you to do something special for yourself. However, to do something special for yourself sometimes means to do something special for someone else. It's not many things that top the feelings you feel when you noticed that you are appreciated, that you are valued, and that your efforts have helped someone to have a better day, or maybe even a better life. When we help others, it creates a circle of life changes. Due to your good deed, you may forever change someone's life. No matter how big or small your deed is, you will never know how much you may have touched someone's soul. In return, you will feel good, and God will bless you for loving his people as he loves you.

What good deeds can you do?

1.	
2.	
3.	
4.	
5.	

What good deed did you do?

_____

_____

_____

_____

_____

How did the receiver react?

_____

_____

_____

_____

_____

_____

How did/do you feel?

_____

_____

_____

_____

_____

_____

Bible verses to meditate on that will further help with this topic:

- Each one must give as he has decided in his heart, not reluctantly or under compulsion, for God loves a cheerful giver. **2 Corinthians 9:7**
- Give, and it will be given to you. Good measure, pressed down, shaken together, running over, will be put into your lap. For with the measure you use it will be measured back to you." **Luke 6:38**
- But Peter said, "I have no silver and gold, but what I do have I give to you. In the name of Jesus Christ of Nazareth, rise up and walk!" **Acts 3:6**

- Not looking to your own interests but each of you to the interests of the others. **Philippians 2:4**

Chapter 9 A little more Help

You're pretty much on your way off to a great journey, but before your done with this book I thought it would be fitting to leave you with a meal plan, grocery list, basic recipes, workouts, S.M.A.R.T Goals, and weekly schedule to start you on your way. If you're interested in supplements to help you with your weight loss journey be sure to check out www.modere.com/1180020 for natural products. The system that I am on that has helped me lose my most recent 50 pounds is called the Lean Sculpting System. I enjoy the Coconut Lime and Chocolate Flavors. Be sure to use my Code 1180020 to receive my discount.

Meal Plans:

I myself am a very sporadic eater. Meaning, I'm the type to take a lunch to work but wind up eating something else. For me, I had to learn to eat what I like and want. If I forced myself to eat something different, the craving would still remain. Sometimes I found myself eating both the wanted and the unwanted food. So, to save my calories I eat what I like. Now by no way am I saying that I eat pizza and snickers all day. Trust if I could lose weight by doing so… I would!!! I treat myself like the children, I give myself options, but all options are within the agreement of me reaching my goals. Let's take your children for example. You have your daughter and you guys are heading to a fancy dinner. She is 8 years old, so you pick out her clothes, but she chooses what she wants to wear. You pick out a nice gold dress and a nice pink dress (lol I hope she is the girly type) She now has the option to choose from these two appropriate dresses. She does not get to choose her blue jean shorts with her favorite butterfly tie in the back shirt.

So, going back to the food. I give myself healthy options to choose from. My favorite food is Macaroni and Cheese and it is not appropriate for everyday eating. So instead of Mac and Cheese, maybe I'll have cauliflower and cheese. If you like to plan out your meals and prepare ahead of time here are some examples. However, if you are sporadic like me. Pick and choose a few of these meals and keep the ingredients in your home to use as needed. That's another thing, the items in which I love, but should not eat often. I do not keep them in my house for at hand access. This way I will have to go to the store and buy it. When I do buy it, I generally only buy for that one serving to help limit temptation.

For me, when it comes to making good food choices, I find that I do better when I do different food challenges. The challenges create small goals that can be fun and quickly obtained. Try different challenges until you find the eating habits that you can do for life so that you reach and maintain your goals.

Here is an example of an ideal meal plan that I would use. It has a healthy combination of protein, complex carbs, and fiber. Your serving size will depend on your daily caloric intake needs (see Chapter 3 to find your caloric needs). I often Intermittent Fast (IF) as also discussed in chapter 3. Also if you find that you are full, you do not need to eat each meal. However, if you are hungry please eat! To starve yourself is not to lose weight. Your body needs food for fuel. It's just a matter of giving it the right things... Also, feel free to think outside the box. Have dinner for breakfast or breakfast for dinner. It is more important to focus on your overall daily intake... Meaning if you have an 1800 caloric intake need, but you are not a breakfast person don't force yourself to eat a heavy breakfast. Especially if you know that you are a late-night eater. Know your body and you're eating habits.

Sample Meal Plan

	Monday	Tuesday	Wednesday	Thursday	Friday	Saturday	Sunday
Breakfast	Overnight Oats	Greek Yogurt and Banana	Eggs and Bacon with fruit	Greek Yogurt with Granola and eggs	Cereal w/ almond milk	Turkey and Cheese Omelet w/ Spinach	Overnight Oats
Snack	Peanut Butter and Apple	Boil Egg	SF Jell-O w/ Whip Cream	Strawberries	Cucumber Slices w/ Lemon Pepper	Almond Butter and Celery	Apple
Lunch	Tuna Wraps	Chicken Salad	Avocado Toast	Cucumber Salad w/ Avocado	Air Fryer Fish with Sweet Potatoes Fries	Cheeseburger Lettuce wrap w/ avocado	Chili
Snack	Cashews and Cheese	Cucumber and Avocado	Boiled Eggs	Almond Butter and Carrots	Boiled Egg And Avocado	Watermelon	Boiled Eggs
Dinner	Meat Loaf w/ Cauliflower Mashed Potatoes	Spaghetti Squash Boat	Chicken Alfredo (Using Multigrain Pasta and sauce on the side)	Chicken Salad	Shrimp, and Brown Rice Stir Fry	Chili	Baked Chicken, Broccoli, And Cheesy Quinoa
Dessert	SF Jell-O w/ Whip Cream	Cottage Cheese and Strawberries	Apple w/ melted peanut butter and nuts	Mix in Season Fruit Salad	Seasonal Fruit Salad	Cottage Cheese w/ Pepper	LC Greek Yogurt

(SF)- Sugar-Free

(LC)- Low Carb

Grocery List

The below grocery list is foods that are needed to make the above meal plan. Please only buy what you plan to eat and plan meals ahead to avoid spending unnecessary money.

Fruit	Meat	Dairy	Other
Strawberries	Tuna (canned in water)	Cheddar Cheese	Unsweetened Almond Milk
Apples	Hamburger Patty	Feta Cheese	Maple Syrup
Fresh/Frozen Mixed Fruit	Bacon	Eggs	Vanilla Abstract
Bananas	Ground Turkey	Greek Yogurt	Peanut Butter
Watermelon	Chicken Breast	Cottage Cheese	Mayonnaise
Avocados	Fish (Tilapia)	Cream Cheese	Mustard
Cucumbers	Ground Beef	Heavy Cream	Ketchup
Tomato	Shrimp		Butter
	Bacon	**Grains**	SF Jell-O
Veggies	Sliced Turkey	Rollin Oats	Cool Whip
Spinach		Chia Seeds	Spaghetti Sauce
Celery	**Nuts**	Wheat Bread	Alfredo Sauce
Lettuce Wrap	Cashews	Multi-Gran Pasta	Granola
Yellow Onion	Peanuts	Multi-Gran Cereal	Almond Butter
Carrots	Almonds	Sweet Potato	Salad Dressing
Cauliflower		Brown Rice	Lemon Pepper
Spring Mix Lettuce		Quinoa in Bag	Chili Seasoning
Broccoli		Red Kidney Beans	Olive Oil
Green Peppers		Low Carb Tortilla Soft Wrap	
Green Onion			
Spaghetti Squash			

<u>Recipes</u>

Avocado Toast

Ingredients

One 8-ounce ripe avocado, halved, pitted and peeled

Fine salt and freshly ground black pepper

4 slices whole grain or whole wheat bread

2 tablespoons extra-virgin olive oil or unsalted butter, softened

Flaky sea salt, for serving

Sprinkled Feta Cheese

Crushed red pepper flakes, optional

Directions

1. Mash the avocado with a fork in a bowl until chunky. Season with salt and black pepper.

2. Toast the bread until browned and crisp. Lightly brush the toasts with oil, and season with fine salt and pepper. Divide the mashed avocado evenly among the toasts, and top with more flaky sea salt, feta cheese, more black pepper, and red pepper flakes; if using.

Overnight Oats

Ingredients

1/2 cup almond milk

1/3 old-fashioned rolled oats

1/3 cup Greek yogurt, optional

1 teaspoon chia seeds, optional but highly recommended

1/2 banana (sliced)

3 Strawberries (sliced)

Directions

1. Add milk, oats, yogurt, chia seeds, strawberries, and banana to a jar or container and give them a good stir. Refrigerate overnight or for at least 5 hours.

2. In the morning, add additional liquid if you'd like. Once you achieve the desired consistency, top with fruit, nuts, seeds, granola, liquid lipo, or vanilla extract.

Cheesy Quinoa Casserole

Ingredients

3 cups cooked quinoa

1/3 cup milk

3/4 cup shredded cheddar cheese

1/2 cup cream cheese

Shredded basil or parsley or another herb for the top

Directions

Preheat the oven to 350 degrees. Grease an 8x8 baking dish and set aside.

1. In a pan over medium-high heat, heat the milk, cream cheese, and cheddar cheese (save some for the top of the dish), stirring until melted, about 1-2 minutes. Add the quinoa and seasoning. Stir together until combined and creamy.

2. Add the quinoa mix to the baking dish and spread until even on the top. Sprinkle the rest of the cheese on top and bake for 15 minutes.

3. Remove from heat and allow to sit for 5 minutes. Top with shredded basil or parsley or another chopped herb.

Keto Chocolate Cookies (all of these ingredients are not listed on the grocery list)

Ingredients
1 cup almond flour
1/4 cup coconut flour

1 stick (8 tablespoons) unsalted butter, at room temperature

1/2 cup erythritol

2 ounces cream cheese, at room temperature

1/2 teaspoon almond extract

1 large egg

1/2 cup sliced almonds

Directions

1. Mix together the almond and coconut flours in a bowl.
2. Combine the butter and erythritol in a different bowl and beat with an electric mixer until light and fluffy for about 2 to 3 minutes. Add the cream cheese and continue to beat until smooth, about 1 minute more. Add the almond extract and egg and beat until combined. Add the flour mixture and continue beating until just combined and smooth. Gently fold in the almonds.
3. Place the mixture onto a piece of parchment or wax paper and, using the paper, mold the dough into a log. Wrap the log in plastic wrap and refrigerate until firm, at least 1 hour.
4. Position an oven rack in the center of the oven and preheat to 350 degrees F. Line a baking sheet with parchment.
5. Slice the dough into 1/2-inch-thick slices and place on the prepared baking sheet. Bake until the edges are golden brown for 18 to 20 minutes. Let cool before serving; the cookies will firm up as they cool down.

<u>Workouts</u>

Below you will find two simple exercises that you can do from the comfort of your home. For demonstration and videos of my full workouts please be sure to check out my YouTube Channel @Clarissa Young. Once on the channel please be sure to like and subscribe to my page.

Strength Workout

1. **Warmup**: March, Dance, or Stretch (3 to 5 Minutes)

2. **Squats**: Rep 1 (20) Rep 2 (15) Rep 3 (10) (to increase intensity hold for 10 seconds or Pulsate for 5 counts)

3. **Ab Rotations:** 20 full rotation, 15 half rotation each side, 10 full rotations

4. **Triceps**: (Ski Position) 20 simultaneous arms, 10 single arms, 20 alternate arms

5. **Squats:** Rep 1 (20) Rep 2 (15) Rep 3 (10) (hold for 10 seconds, Pulsate for 5 count)

6. **Ab Rotations:** 20 full rotation, 15 half rotation each side, 10 full rotations

7. **Lateral Raises**: (Ski Position) 20 simultaneous arms, 10 single arms, 20 alternate

8. **Squats**: Rep 1 (20) Rep 2 (15) Rep 3 (10) (hold for 10 seconds, Pulsate for 5 count)

9. **Ab Rotations:** 20 full rotation, 15 half rotation each side, 10 full rotations

10. **Drop weights**: 20 sets bend forward for weights, stand up straight, push weights up, drop weights

11. **Lunges**: 10 each leg x 3

12. **Ab Rotations**: 20 full rotation, 15 half rotation each side, 10 full rotations

13. **Cool Down**: March, Dance, or Stretch at a slow pace (3 to 5 minutes)

Cardio HIIT

Each exercise will be done for one minute followed by a 30-second break. Give it your all during each rep. Each exercise will be repeated 3 times. Feel free to check your app store for free Tabata or HIIT timers.

1. Warmup: Freestyle (Walk or Dance... get the heart rate up 4 to 8 minutes)
2. Side Shuffle Touch (4 counts)
3. Squatted Speed Bag
4. Front/Back Kicks
5. Chops
6. Front Punches (High Punches and Mid Punches)
7. Dip Blocks
8. Jump Rope *Repeat Rep (2-8) 3 to 5 times*
9. Cool Down: Stretch (3 to 5 minutes)

S.M.A.R.T Goals

All goals have a final destination in mind. However, the most important key to getting you to your destination is the route taken. When making goals you can use the below chart for a tool in creating attainable goals.***

S	M	A	R	T
Specific	Measurable	Attainable	Realistic	Time-Bound
"I want to lose 20 pounds"	"I will use the scale to track my weight"	"I will aim to lose 2-3 pounds a week"	"I am 250 pounds and I want to weigh 230 pounds"	"I am to lose 20 pounds in 10 weeks"

***Once your goals are mapped out, be sure to write down the necessary steps that you plan to take to obtain your goals. What will you eat, will you exercise, or will you do self-development?

Blank Weekly Schedules

Time	Sunday	Monday	Tuesday	Wednesday	Thursday	Friday	Saturday
12:00 am							
1:00 am							
2:00 am							
3:00 am							
4:00 am							
5:00 am							
6:00 am							
7:00 am							
8:00 am							
9:00 am							
10:00 am							
11:00 am							
12:00 pm							
1:00 pm							
2:00 pm							

3:00 pm							
4:00 pm							
5:00 pm							
6:00 pm							
7:00 pm							
8:00 pm							
9:00 pm							
10:00 pm							
11:00 pm							

Blank Weekly Schedules

Time	Sunday	Monday	Tuesday	Wednesday	Thursday	Friday	Saturday
12:00 am							
1:00 am							
2:00 am							
3:00 am							
4:00 am							
5:00 am							
6:00 am							
7:00 am							
8:00 am							
9:00 am							
10:00 am							
11:00 am							
12:00 pm							
1:00 pm							
2:00 pm							

3:00 pm						
4:00 pm						
5:00 pm						
6:00 pm						
7:00 pm						
8:00 pm						
9:00 pm						
10:00 pm						
11:00 pm						

Blank Weekly Schedules

Time	Sunday	Monday	Tuesday	Wednesday	Thursday	Friday	Saturday
12:00 am							
1:00 am							
2:00 am							
3:00 am							
4:00 am							
5:00 am							
6:00 am							
7:00 am							
8:00 am							
9:00 am							
10:00 am							
11:00 am							
12:00 pm							
1:00 pm							
2:00 pm							

3:00 pm							
4:00 pm							
5:00 pm							
6:00 pm							
7:00 pm							
8:00 pm							
9:00 pm							
10:00 pm							
11:00 pm							

Blank Weekly Schedules

Time	Sunday	Monday	Tuesday	Wednesday	Thursday	Friday	Saturday
12:00 am							
1:00 am							
2:00 am							
3:00 am							
4:00 am							
5:00 am							
6:00 am							
7:00 am							
8:00 am							
9:00 am							
10:00 am							
11:00 am							
12:00 pm							
1:00 pm							
2:00 pm							

3:00 pm						
4:00 pm						
5:00 pm						
6:00 pm						
7:00 pm						
8:00 pm						
9:00 pm						
10:00 pm						
11:00 pm						

Blank Weekly Schedules

Time	Sunday	Monday	Tuesday	Wednesday	Thursday	Friday	Saturday
12:00 am							
1:00 am							
2:00 am							
3:00 am							
4:00 am							
5:00 am							
6:00 am							
7:00 am							
8:00 am							
9:00 am							
10:00 am							
11:00 am							
12:00 pm							
1:00 pm							
2:00 pm							

3:00 pm							
4:00 pm							
5:00 pm							
6:00 pm							
7:00 pm							
8:00 pm							
9:00 pm							
10:00 pm							
11:00 pm							

Blank Weekly Schedules

Time	Sunday	Monday	Tuesday	Wednesday	Thursday	Friday	Saturday
12:00 am							
1:00 am							
2:00 am							
3:00 am							
4:00 am							
5:00 am							
6:00 am							
7:00 am							
8:00 am							
9:00 am							
10:00 am							
11:00 am							
12:00 pm							
1:00 pm							
2:00 pm							

3:00 pm							
4:00 pm							
5:00 pm							
6:00 pm							
7:00 pm							
8:00 pm							
9:00 pm							
10:00 pm							
11:00 pm							

3 John 1:2

Beloved, I pray that all may go well with you and that you may be in good health, as it goes well with your soul.

Made in the USA
Columbia, SC
21 September 2019